New Kittredge Shakespeare

William Shakespeare

THE TRAGEDY OF
MACBETH

William Shakespeare

THE TRAGEDY OF
MACBETH

Editor
Annalisa Castaldo
University

Series Editor
James H. Lake
Louisiana State University,
Shreveport

To my husband, Alex.

TABLE OF CONTENTS

Publisher's Note

George Lyman Kittredge's insightful editions of Shakespeare have endured in part because of his eclecticism, his diversity of interests, and his wide-ranging accomplishments — all of which are reflected in the valuable notes in each volume. The plays in the *New Kittredge Shakespeare* series retain the original Kittredge notes and introductions, changed or augmented only when some modernization seems necessary. These new editions also include introductory essays by contemporary editors, notes on the plays as they have been performed on stage and film, and additional student materials.

These plays are being made available by Focus Publishing with the permission of the Kittredge heirs.

Ron Pullins, Publisher
Newburyport, 2007

Acknowledgments

I would like to thank Ron Pullins and James Lake for offering me the opportunity to work on this project. I am also deeply grateful to Kathleen Brophy, the wonderful editor who guided a first timer through the process of making a book. Finally, I am grateful for the help of the Widener librarians, who tirelessly ran down the materials I needed.

Annalisa Castaldo
July, 2007

Introduction to the Kittredge Edition

For the text of MACBETH the only authority is the First Folio. This prints what is obviously an acting version of the play, somewhat changed from its original form. Hecate is an intrusive character, quite foreign to Shakespeare's conception of the powers and attributes of the Weird Sisters: the whole of the fifth scene in Act 3 is a manifest interpolation; and the same is true of 4.1.39–43, 125–132, which must stand or fall with that scene. Two stage directions in the Folio (3.5.33; 4.1.43) call for songs that are preserved in Middleton's tragicomedy *The Witch*. This fact, as well as the character of Hecate in Middleton, suggests that he may have been the playwright employed to revise Shakespeare's MACBETH in an operatic spirit, out of harmony with the original design.

There is no decisive evidence for date. Outside limits are 1603 (the accession of James I)[1] and 1610, when Simon Forman attended a performance of MACBETH at the Globe. 1610 is manifestly several years too late for the composition of the play, as both style and metre show. To fix upon a year within the limits many supposed criteria have been cited—all of them interesting, but none of them decisive. When James I was approaching the North Gate of Oxford, on his visit to the city in 1605 (August 27), "tres quasi Sibyllae" emerged from St. John's College, "as if from a wood," and saluted the King, the Queen, and the Princes Henry and Charles, with a few Latin verses composed by Dr. Matthew Gwinne. The First Sibyl mentioned the prophecy spoken by the Weird Sisters to Banquo and designated King James as Banquo's descendant. He was greeted also as a ruler of Scotland, England, and Ireland—and likewise as monarch of Britain (now united), Ireland, and France (cf. 4.1.121). But Shakespeare needed no hint from Gwinne for the Weird Sisters. They are central figures of the Macbeth legend as told by Holinshed, with whose standard work he had been familiar for more than a dozen years. The farmer (or other speculator in wheat) "that hang'd himself on th' expectation of plenty" was a stock figure as early as the thirteenth century and is not to be connected especially with the price of wheat in 1606. The Porter's "equivocator" need not involve an allusion to Garnet, who was tried on March 28, 1606. Possible echoes of MACBETH in almost contemporary plays are interesting but by no means conclusive.

---

1   James I succeeded Elizabeth on March 24, 1603, and was crowned on July 25.

Everything considered, Malone's date for MACBETH, 1606, has stood all tests for more than a century. Style and metre fit this date, but 1605 is also possible; for we cannot be quite sure whether MACBETH came just before *King Lear* or just after it.

For the plot Shakespeare had recourse to the second edition of Raphael Holinshed's *Chronicle* (1587). Since he was writing a tragedy and not a "history," he did not hesitate to take liberties. The rebellion of Macdonwald and the invasion of "Sweno the Norways' king" are brought together. Banquo, King James's fictitious ancestor, is represented as a loyal subject, whereas in Holinshed he is Macbeth's chief ally in the attack on Duncan. For the murder of Duncan, Shakespeare has used Holinshed's account of the murder of King Duff by Donwald, which includes the drugging of the chamberlains and the prodigies described in 2.4. The voice that cried "Sleep no more!" was apparently suggested by what Holinshed tells of the dream of King Kenneth III. The Weird Sisters disappear from Holinshed immediately after their meeting with Macbeth upon the blasted heath. The warning to "beware Macduff" (4.1.71) is given by "certeine wizzards, in whose words [Macbeth] put great confidence"; the prophecies concerning "none of woman born" and Birnam Wood (4.1.80, 92–94) are made by "a certeine witch, whome hee had in great trust."[2]

Holinshed's authority was the *Scotorum Historiae* [History of Scotland] of Hector Boece (born *ca.* 1465, died 1536), which goes back to John Fordun's *Scotichronicon* (written in the latter part of the fourteenth century) and to Andrew of Wyntown's *Cronykil* (finished *ca.* 1424). The material combines a modicum of sober history with much ancient legend and considerable out-and-out fiction. To sift the actual facts from this conglomerate is a fascinating problem for investigators, but does not much concern the Shakespearean student. One may note, however, that Duncan's reign was A.D. 1034–1040 and Macbeth's A.D. 1040–1057. Macbeth seems to have had some title to the crown, but just what it was cannot be determined. He was certainly not Duncan's cousin, as Holinshed (following Boece) and Shakespeare (following Holinshed) represent. He asserted his claim, after the fashion of those times, by attacking Duncan with an armed troop at a place near Elgin. Duncan was killed, but whether or not he fell by Macbeth's own hand is uncertain. In 1054 Macbeth was defeated, probably at Dunsinane, by Siward (not accompanied by Malcolm). He maintained himself in the north until August, 1057, when he fell at Lumphanan in a battle with Malcolm. Banquo and Fleance are unhistorical characters who make their first appearances in Boece. Macduff is likewise fictitious—at least in any such rôle as he plays in Holinshed and Shakespeare. Macdonwald and Cawdor were also brought into the story by Boece.

The historical Macbeth was a sane and beneficent ruler. Fordun, on the contrary, represents him as a savage tyrant. Boece combines these two characters,

---

2   The earliest writer to attach these two prophecies to Macbeth's history is Wyntown (*Cronykil, ca.* 1420; vi, 18, 1929–1930, 2207–2228, ed. Laing, II, 130, 138–139). According to him, the former was uttered by the devil, who was Macbeth's father. The source of the latter he does not specify, but it seems to have been the same demon. Both accord with widespread folktales. For a thorough treatment of the Macbeth legend see Ernst Kröger, *Die Sage von Macbeth bis zu Shakspere,* 1904.

and Holinshed follows Boece. Macbeth, he tells us, was "somewhat cruell of nature," yet for ten years he ruled wisely and well.

In delineating Macbeth's character, Shakespeare departed widely from Holinshed. In the first scene of the play we learn nothing about him but his name. The next scene is definitely expository. From beginning to end it is a laudation of Macbeth— "brave Macbeth (well he deserves that name)"; "valour's minion" (or darling); "Bellona's bridegroom." The Sergeant praises him, expressing the sentiments of the army and the common people; then Ross enters and voices the admiration of the peers; and finally King Duncan closes the scene with a kind of suspiration— "noble Macbeth." The words of Macbeth to his wife, soon after, fitly describe the tenor of the whole— "golden opinions from all sorts of people."[3] The impression that the expository scene makes upon us is decisive: Macbeth is the first of the Scottish nobles, beloved and admired by everybody, from the rank and file of the army to the King himself—a great soldier, a true patriot, a loyal subject. He is contrasted with "the merciless Macdonwald" and with "that most disloyal traitor, the Thane of Cawdor." Such was Macbeth before the "supernatural soliciting" that determined his later career.

A second piece of evidence is highly significant, for it concerns two qualities not touched upon in the expository scene. It is Lady Macbeth's soliloquy after she reads her husband's letter. She knows him well. He is "not without ambition," but his ambition is of the honorable kind. The thought of kingship attracts him, but he will shrink from achieving the crown by any deed that will stain his conscience: "What thou wouldst highly, that wouldst thou holily." And besides, he is gentle and kindly by temperament, and "the nearest way"—which to her straightforward feminine logic is the only way—will horrify him. Lady Macbeth, then, adds to what we have learned in the expository scene—to valor and loyalty and patriotism—the qualities of a scrupulous conscience and a humane and kindly temper. This last trait, one remembers, has often been noted—to the amazement of superficial observers of human nature—in great military heroes, veritable thunderbolts of war. That the Lady is right in her analysis is confirmed by much circumstantial evidence: by Macbeth's horror when the thought of murder first darts into his mind; by his vacillation before the deed;[4] by the hallucinations that precede and follow it; by his naïve wonder that he "could not say 'Amen!' when they did say 'God bless us!'" ; by his remorse. Even the savagery of his later career, which has deterred some critics from accepting the unimpeachable evidence of his wife, is in fact a confirmation. A savage may be little the worse for a murder or two, but Macbeth has subverted the very foundations of his being. He has "cursed his better angel from his side and fallen to reprobance."

---

3   1.7.33. This phrase would be almost enough to prove the genuineness of the second scene, even if that scene were not, as it is, vitally necessary to the understanding of the drama.

4   Note especially the antithesis of ambition and pity in Macbeth's soliloquy in 1.7.1–28. Cf. the use of "unfortunate" in 4.1.152.

Macbeth is blessed—and cursed—with an imagination of extraordinary power, which visualizes to the verge of delirium. Every idea that enters his mind takes instant visible shape: he *sees* what another would merely *think*. And this poetic vision (which at the outset so presented the hideousness of murder as almost to thwart his purpose) comes later to his aid. It enables him to think and speak about himself as if he were a spectator at his own tragedy, and so he finds a refuge from the direct contemplation of fact. Thus he grows stronger and more resolute as fate closes in upon him, and is never greater than in the desperate valour that marks his end.

The rôle and character of Lady Macbeth are barely suggested by Holinshed. He tells us that Macbeth was "greatlie incouraged" by "the woords of the thre weird sisters" to "vsurpe the kingdome by force." "But," he adds, "speciallie his wife lay sore vpon him to attempt the thing, as she that was verie ambitious, burning in vnquenchable desire to beare the name of a queene." That is all: Holinshed never mentions her again.

Lady Macbeth, then, is Shakespeare's own creation. Like all normal women, she is ambitious, but her ambition is rather for her husband than herself. It is for his head that "fate and metaphysical aid" have destined "the golden round" (1.5.26–31); her task is to remove the obstacles inherent in his nature. With her, to see is to purpose and to purpose is to proceed right onward with an eye single to the end in view: "the nearest way" is the only way. She sways Macbeth by her strength of will and her feminine charm. She coaxes him and soothes him and taunts him, as the occasion may require; but she does not bully him as Goneril bullies Albany. Their devotion to each other is manifest in every word they speak. Their marriage is the perfect union of complementary natures, each supplying those qualities that the other lacks. Thus the climax of their tragic history is Macbeth's apathy when he hears that his wife is dead.

Lady Macbeth's strength resides in her nervous force and the terrible simplicity of her point of view. She is no creature of heroic frame.[5] And she has overestimated her nervous energy. It might have sufficed to carry her, unshaken, through the consequences of any act that she could have executed alone. It could not suffice when constantly drawn upon to support and animate her husband, who seems to her to be going mad. Hence the infinite pathos of her final breakdown when the bloody instructions have returned to plague the inventors.

For the Weird Sisters in their relation to Macbeth the earliest authority is Wyntown, who makes them appear to him in a dream. Their name comes from the Anglo-Saxon *wyrd,* "fate."

In adopting the term "Weird Sisters" from Holinshed Shakespeare was obviously adopting also Holinshed's definition— "the goddesses of destiny." The Weird Sisters, then, are the Norns of Scandinavian mythology. The Norns were goddesses who shaped beforehand the life of every man. Sometimes they came in the night and stood by the cradle of the newborn child, uttering their decrees; for their office was not to prophesy only, but to determine. Sometimes they were met in wild places

---

5   See 3.2.45 ("dearest chuck"); 5.1.38–39 ("this little hand"); and note her swoon in 2.3.108–109.

and at unexpected moments. Once they were seen in a remote den in the woods, weaving the visible web of doom on the day of a great battle in which many perished. Now they appear as the guardians of a favourite hero; again, they are hostile, and bent only on a man's destruction: but always and everywhere they are great and terrible powers, from whose mandate there is no appeal. In all probability, their attachment to the story goes back to the time of Macbeth himself. Their presence is due to the large infusion of Norse blood in the Scottish race, and their function is in full accord with the doctrines of Norse heathendom. That function, then, was an essential element in the history of Macbeth as it came into Shakespeare's hands. These were not ordinary witches or seeresses. They were great powers of destiny, great ministers of fate. They had determined the past; they governed the present; they not only foresaw the future, but decreed it. All this was manifest to Shakespeare as he read the chronicle. He assimilated the conception in its entirety by a single act of sympathetic imagination; and he reproduced it in his tragedy, not in any literal or dogmatic shape, but coloured and intensified by his creative genius, and modified by his trained sense of what it is possible to represent upon the actual stage.

Thus the tragedy of MACBETH is inevitably fatalistic, but Shakespeare attempts no solution of the problem of free will and predestination. It is not his office to make a contribution to philosophy or theology. He never gives us the impression that a man is not responsible for his own acts. "It will have blood, they say; blood will have blood."

George Lyman Kittredge

INTRODUCTION TO THE FOCUS EDITION

In *Macbeth*, Shakespeare explores as fully as possible the corruption of the human soul. Macbeth begins the plays as a hero—he is the triumphant general who defeats two armies and the favorite noble of a grateful king who loads him with honors. Yet the instant after the Weird Sisters present him with the promise of the crown, Macbeth assumes that his path must be bloody. While the Weird Sisters have only assured him he will be "king hereafter" (a reasonable suggestion in an elected rather than inherited monarchy), Macbeth's response is to wonder why his imagination conjures "that suggestion/Whose horrid image" frightens him so completely. The suggestion that immediately presents itself to him is that he "catch the nearest way" and take the throne by force. From this moment, he is dragged inexorably downward despite the struggles of his own conscience. Critics continue to argue over whether Macbeth is controlled by the Weird Sisters, or his wife, or both, as well as whether he has ambitions towards the crown even before hearing the prophecies. The point, however, is not that there is a single right answer, but that Shakespeare has carefully arranged events so that we never quite know. As with real life, there is a constant battle between the belief that the individual has free will and that he is shaped by his environment, between the idea that single events or choices change everything and the idea that everything is fated to turn out the way it does.

Perhaps this is why *Macbeth* has a history of being an unlucky play, with productions resulting in injury or other disasters—the themes are too close to the messy unpredictability of real life. And just like real life, the emphasis and importance of events and characters depends on who is telling the story. Some interpretations make the Weird Sisters masters of fate and the human characters mere puppets. Others shift the focus to Lady Macbeth and make her the dominant partner who bullies an essentially noble Macbeth into a horrible act. Still others point to Macbeth's warrior nature, so strongly emphasized in 1.2, and consider him a completely independent agent. None of these readings is wrong, but none is entirely right, and thus the play continues to fascinate audiences and scholars alike.

To balance such murky themes and motivations, Shakespeare cleverly made the motifs exceptionally strong and clear. Certain images or ideas are repeated over and over, grounding the play from first to last. The most notable of these images is blood.

From the first line of the second scene "What bloody man is that?" to Macbeth's words to Macduff in the final act, "my soul/is too much charged with blood of thine already," the word echoes through the play. The physicality of death is dwelt on as in no other play—bloody daggers (both real and hallucinated), murderers spotted with blood, bloody ghosts—as Macbeth says "It will have blood; blood will have blood" and "it" seems to refer not just to the specific murder of Banquo, but the corrupted world of *Macbeth* and the play itself. In all, the word "blood" or variants appear over fifty times.

In 4.1, the Weird Sisters produce a vision of a bloody child, thus linking the motif of blood with that of the child. Children, as symbols of innocence and of the future, are of vital importance to *Macbeth*. Real children—in the form of Fleance, who escapes murder, Macduff's son, who does not, and Macbeth's, whose absence allows the prophecies to go forward—are only the beginning. Lady Macbeth uses the horrific image of dashing out the brains of a nursing baby; two of the three apparitions the Weird Sisters show Macbeth involve children and, in the end, Macduff is able to defeat Macbeth because of how he entered the world: "untimely ripped" from his mother's womb rather than born as a normal child.

The opposite of innocent childhood is corrupted adulthood, and as much as the play emphasizes the possibilities of children, it is obsessed with defining what a man actually is. Contemplating murder, Macbeth says, "I may do all that may become a man/Who dares do more is done" and yet he goes on to do more, to commit murder. Yet perhaps murder is the very thing that makes a man. Certainly Macbeth begins the play praised for his ability to kill, and even at the end of the play there is a reluctant admiration for his fearlessness. When Macbeth asks the Murderers if they will be revenged upon Banquo, they respond "We are men," meaning that to be a man is to answer (apparent) insult with violence. When Macduff hears that his wife and children have been slain, Malcolm tells him to "Bear it like a man;" that is, to focus on killing Macbeth rather than grieving his loss. Even the minor characters echo this idea. Siward, on being told his son is dead, asks only whether he died fighting rather than fleeing. Reassured that he died "like a man," Siward is content.

The final motif, and the one which brings all the others together and returns them to the shifting meanings of the play as a whole, is that of equivocation, "the fiend that lies like truth." Shakespeare's contemporaries had a keen interest in the idea of equivocation—saying something that is likely to be understood one way, while actually meaning something else—because of its use by Catholics. Those arrested by the Protestant government used equivocal statements to protect themselves from persecution without actually denying their faith. To the Protestant majority, equivocation appeared to be proof that Catholicism and Catholics were corrupted and interested in appearance rather than truth.

Shakespeare expanded this fascination beyond its specifically religious sense, recognizing that much of what seems true is ambiguous at best. The Weird Sisters open the play chanting "Fair is foul and foul is fair" and the play ends with a victory that is not really a victory, since Banquo's children, not Malcolm's, have been foretold as the future of Scotland. The Weird Sisters' prophecies come true, but in ways that neither Macbeth nor the audience expects. J.R.R. Tolkein was famously so upset at the way the prophecies worked out that in his "Lord of the Rings" trilogy he created the Ents as a real moving forest, and had the Nazgul Lord defeated by the disguised Eowyn, a woman, who is literally "no man." While many have agreed that Shakespeare's working out of the prophecies is particularly unsatisfying, the point, in fact, is that meaning arises not from events, but from the way we view and react to those events. Shakespeare wasn't trying (and failing) to be clever; he was pointing out that life does not follow the neat tracks we assume it will.

Macbeth is short, action packed, and full of special effects to delight audiences. It was probably written to curry favor with the new king, James I, who was Scottish himself, and fascinated by witches. In lesser hands, Macbeth would have been nothing more than a pawn, the Weird Sisters purely evil and the final battle the total success of the heroes. But instead of simply creating an early version of the action film, Shakespeare shaped an investigation of human nature as messy and complicated as human nature itself.

Performance History

Although we do not know the exact date of *Macbeth*'s composition, the subject matter makes clear that it was composed to appeal to a very specific audience—the new monarch, James I of England and IV of Scotland. The setting—Scotland—the characters—especially that of Banquo, James' supposed ancestor—and the theme—control of both man and fate by the supernatural, an obsession with James—make clear that the original audience was indeed the King. The play was immediately popular, but authorities cancelled the run after two performances because it was considered unfit for princes to be portrayed on stage. The real reason may have been that staging a regicide (even offstage) was more than James, who had already survived several attempts on his life and who was terrified of assassination, was willing to countenance. Whatever the reason, *Macbeth* would only be kept off the stage by governmental intervention—the play has remained a popular choice for actors of all levels since it was first staged.

During the later part of the English Civil War and Interregnum, the theaters were closed (1642-1660). When Charles II was restored to the throne, the theaters were reopened and Shakespeare's plays were divided between the two licenced companies, with *Macbeth* going to Sir William Davenant. Davenent, along with others, was perfectly content to "update" Shakespeare. Davenant rewrote much of Shakespeare's language, cut the Porter scene, added a scene in which Lady Macbeth is haunted by the Ghost of Banquo and added four new scenes featuring Lady Macduff, including a scene in which the Witches visit Macduff, and Lady Macduff urges her husband to ignore their prophecies and trust in God. The additions make Macduff a more worthy adversary and Lady Macduff a saintly foil for the evil Lady Macbeth. Davenant's version was hugely popular and held the stage for 70 years. It was only gradually that the *Macbeth* that Shakespeare wrote would retake the stage.

Another alteration that apparently dates from very early is the role of the Weird Sisters as musical interlude rather than unnerving supernatural force. The songs the Weird Sisters sing in 3.5 and 4.1 are not by Shakespeare, but rather from Thomas Middleton's *The Witch*. Until well into the nineteenth century, the Weird Sisters (more commonly called witches in these performances) ranged from comic relief to excuses to demonstrate the latest in theater technology.

The nineteenth century was obsessed with theatrical realism, and in the case of *Macbeth* this meant authentic Scottish dress, backdrops that represented eleventh-century castles, and long battle scenes with, often, dozens of extras. The passion for accuracy did not necessarily extend to the text itself. Charles Kean's 1820 production, for example, included in the playbill a list of the scholarly sources consulted to make sure the production was as historically accurate as possible, but he left out the Porter scene, among others.

In the twentieth century, productions of Shakespeare in general have returned to simpler staging and focus on the language and characters Shakespeare created. Although *Macbeth* is no exception, the supernatural elements continue to attract directors interested in innovation, and great energy has been expended on making realistic ghosts and witches. More important is the way in which the play has, in the last one hundred years, become a favorite means of commenting on politics. Macbeth, Lady Macbeth, Duncan, even Scotland itself can be portrayed as either inherently healthy and moral, destroyed by an external flaw, or corrupted and immoral, doomed from the start. Perhaps the best known example of this was Orson Welles' famous 1936 "Voodoo" *Macbeth* which featured an all-black cast and was set in Haiti as a way to comment on Fascism and the corruption of political systems in general.

The roles of Macbeth and Lady Macbeth are two of the most powerful Shakespeare created, and in each there is a paradox. Macbeth is hailed by all around him as a noble, even heroic figure, and his wife, who should know him best, fears he is "too full o' the milk of human kindness" to murder Duncan. Indeed, at first, Macbeth recoils at the mere thought of murder, but by Act 4, he orders Macduff's entire family slaughtered. Lady Macbeth is often seen, in the words of Malcolm, as "fiend-like," unfeminine and even inhuman. Yet in her great speech to the spirits she asks that she be "unsexed" and she tells Macbeth she knows "how tender 'tis to love the babe that milks [her]." By the end of the play she is wracked with guilt and fear–sleepwalking and eventually committing suicide. Both of the Macbeths undergo profound transformations and it is this vast range in their emotions that draws actors as well as scholars to the roles.

Films and Adaptations

Macbeth is one of Shakespeare's most frequently filmed plays—the supernatural elements seem tailor-made for the special effects of the movies. Therefore this introduction will focus on only a few of the major productions. Likewise, although there are many filmed adaptations of *Macbeth*, only two—*Men of Respect* and *Scotland, PA* will be discussed.

The first important film of *Macbeth* was Orson Welles' 1948 production. As with his other Shakespearean films, Welles drastically cut and rearranged the text, even creating a new character—the Church Father—out of several minor characters. His conception of the Weird Sisters as fog-shrouded, barely human shapes is eerie, and their reappearance at the very end of the play suggests that evil wins out over good. Welles created an impressionistic, even hallucinatory world: Macbeth's castle seems hacked out of rock and not even completely enclosed. Banquo's Ghost as well as the dagger are presented as arising from Macbeth's fevered imagination, and through camera angles Macbeth either towers over his subjects or cowers, fearful and tiny, beneath the sky. While many of the supporting cast are weak, and the decision to insist on Scottish accents throughout results in more than a few laughable moments, the film retains great power and Welles' performance as Macbeth is magnificent.

In 1971 Roman Polanski created a new version of the play, emphasizing brutal realism. In fact, the play opens not with Shakespeare's first scene, but with the aftermath of the battle only described in the play. As the credits roll, the soldiers casually murder the survivors they find on the battlefield. Many scholars have suggested that Roman Polanski created this film in response to the Manson family murder of his wife Sharon Tate. Thus the offstage murders become brutally realistic on screen, the witches border on insanity rather than demonic possession, and Macbeth himself, played by Jon Finch, is young, handsome and athletic enough to make the audience forget for far too long what he is doing. In an unorthodox casting, Lady Macbeth is played by Francesca Annis, young, beautiful and even a bit fragile. She is not the driving force of Macbeth's ambition, but a devoted wife, and the nude sleepwalking scene emphasizes her innocence as much as her beauty.

A stripped-down televised version starring Ian McKellen and Judi Dench was filmed in 1979 and is well worth seeking out. Essentially a filmed version of the stage production created by Trevor Nunn, this is minimalist Shakespeare—black box set, practically no props and neutral costumes. But instead of boredom, the minimalism creates almost unbearable intensity on the psychological torment the Macbeths inflict on themselves through their immoral choices.

Critics sometimes disagree on whether Akira Kurosawa's *Kumonosu jô* (correctly translated *Castle of the Spider's Web* but known in America as *Throne of Blood*) is a production of *Macbeth* or an adaptation of it. Despite the fact that the film is set in Samuri Japan and features not a single word of Shakespeare's language, I find myself in the camp that sees this as the best production of *Macbeth* yet filmed, rather than as an adaptation. Kurosawa has transformed all of Shakespeare's key themes. By viewing the play through the lens of Noh drama, using beautifully framed shots and moments of great stillness, he conveys issues of morality, madness, corruption and power.

Two of the most interesting adaptations of *Macbeth* are *Men of Respect* and *Scotland, PA*. The former is a mafia version, while the latter sets the play in a fast food restaurant during the 1970s. *Men of Respect*, while a flawed film, does a fascinating job of modernizing many of the aspects of the play. For example, Ruthie Battaglia (the Lady Macbeth character) had an abortion at her husband's request, and uses that loss to manipulate him into murder echoing Lady Macbeth's declaration that she would kill her own child if she had sworn an oath like Macbeth's. A fortune teller replaces the Weird Sisters and the prophecy of stars falling from the sky replaces the moving Birnam Wood.

Scotland, PA transposes the story from the level of royalty to that of lower class fast food employees. By deflating the rewards and emphasizing the hapless stupidity of the Macbeths (they accidentally drown Duncan in a fryer, rather than planning to murder him), the film shifts focus from tragedy to black comedy. This shift is especially apparent in the treatment of the supernatural. The witches are three persistently stoned hippies, and it is never clear that they actually exist, since Mac is the only one who sees them, and only when completely drunk.

The Scottish play has been adapted in opera, ballet, novel, and song, and there is always a production of it running somewhere; with *Hamlet* and *Romeo and Juliet* it is one of Shakespeare's most popular plays. *Macbeth* remains immensely powerful no matter the setting. Because the themes are so richly and yet ambiguously universal and the lead roles are so flexible and yet so arresting, actors and directors, audiences and scholars continue to be drawn to the play as inexorably as Macbeth is drawn towards murder.

Annalisa Castaldo, 2007

Editor's Note

Kittredge's editing is wonderfully clear and I have made only minor changes. I have Americanized the spelling throughout, and have modernized punctuation more completely than Kittredge did, to aid readers in understanding the text. In addition, I removed material from the introduction and footnotes which provided linguistic connections to other plays. While this material is of use to scholars, it is often intimidating to students and does not necessarily enrich their understanding of the scene.

Kittredge presented a very specific reading of *Macbeth*, based on viewing the Weird Sisters as aspects of Fate. I have excluded his more directive notes, as I feel that it should be up to the reader how he or she understands a particular scene; the editor may point out details, but should not make absolute pronouncements. I have, however, kept Kittredge's excellent notes about the timing and flow of scenes.

[A.C.]

THE TRAGEDY OF
MACBETH

DRAMATIS PERSONAE

Duncan, King of Scotland

Malcolm,
Donalbain, } his sons.

Macbeth, ⎱ Generals of the
Banquo, ⎰ Scottish Army.

Macduff,
Lenox,
Ross,   Noblemen
Menteith,   of Scotland.
Angus,
Caithness,

Fleance, son to *Banquo.*

Siward, Earl of Northumberland,
      General of the English forces.

Young Siward, his son.

Boy, son to Macduff

A Sergeant.

A Porter.

An Old Man.

An English Doctor.

A Scottish Doctor.

Lady Macbeth.

Lady Macduff.

A Gentlewoman, attending on *Lady*
      Macbeth.

The Weird Sisters.

Hecate.

The Ghost of *Banquo.*

Apparitions.

Lords, Gentlemen, Officers, Murderers,
      Messengers, Attendants.

SCENE.—*Scotland; England.*

1

ACT I

Thunder and lightning. Enter three Witches.

1. WITCH.	When shall we three meet again In thunder, lightning, or in rain?	
2. WITCH.	When the hurlyburly's done, When the battle's lost and won.	
3. WITCH.	That will be ere the set of sun.	5
1. WITCH.	Where the place?	
2. WITCH.	Upon the heath.	
3. WITCH.	There to meet with Macbeth.	
1. WITCH.	I come, Graymalkin!	
2. WITCH.	Paddock calls.	
3. WITCH.	Anon!	

ACT I. SCENE I.

The tragedy plunges, as usual, *in medias res.* The Weird Sisters are at the close of a consultation and about to separate. We infer that they have some design that involves Macbeth; but not until scene 2 do we learn who Macbeth is, or what is meant by "the battle." The place of the scene is not indicated in the Folios. We may imagine any wild and desolate region—not, however, the blasted heath where the Sisters meet Macbeth in scene 3, since that is mentioned as a different place in line 6. In this scene, as elsewhere, we note a gradation in the knowledge of the Weird Sisters. The first asks questions; the second answers; the third gives definite information about the future—namely, that the battle will be over before sunset and that Macbeth will cross a certain heath. 1-2. **When...rain?** When shall we meet again in a storm? Witches and demons were supposed to be particularly active in boisterous weather, which, indeed, was often thought to be caused by their spells (cf. 1.3.10–25; 4.1.52–60). The storm at the outset is symbolic of the whole course of this tempestuous drama. There is a storm on the night of Duncan's murder, and the next day is dark and gloomy (2.3.59–68; 2.4.1–10). When Banquo is attacked (3.3.16) a storm is brewing. Thunder ushers in the Weird Sisters in 4.1.3. **hurlyburly.** The battle described in the next scene is now raging. 8-9. **Graymalkin,** etc. The Weird Sisters are summoned by their "familiars" (attendant spirits), who have been instructed to call when the time comes for their mistresses to depart, each on her own evil errand. One of these demons has the shape of a grey cat, another that of a paddock or toad. The name and shape of the Third Sister's familiar are not mentioned; but he calls, like the others, and she answers "Anon!" i.e., "In a moment!"

---

† The presentation of the witches is a key element of the director's vision of the play. Welles shrouded his witches in fog and drapery, so that they seemed faceless and not quite human, emphasizing his belief that the play was an essential struggle between good and evil. Polanski, on the other hand, made the witches entirely human (even as their varying ages echoed traditions of the Triple Goddess, representing maiden, mother and crone), signaling his view that the action is motivated by human greed and fear, rather than anything supernatural. [A.C.]

| ALL. | Fair is foul, and foul is fair. | 10 |

Hover through the fog and filthy air.   *Exeunt.*

Scene II. [*A camp near Forres.*]†

Alarum within. Enter King [Duncan], Malcolm, Donalbain, Lennox, *with* Attendants, *meeting a bleeding* Sergeant.

KING.   What bloody man is that? He can report,
               As seemeth by his plight, of the revolt
               The newest state.

MAL.   This is the sergeant
               Who like a good and hardy soldier fought
               'Gainst my captivity. Hail, brave friend!   5
               Say to the King the knowledge of the broil
               As thou didst leave it.

10-11. Fair is foul, etc. Fair weather and good deeds are foul to the Weird Sisters, and only foul things are beautiful. Their principle is that of Milton's Satan— "Evil, be thou my good."

Scene II.
This scene takes place on the same day as scene 1. We hear full details of the double victory won by Macbeth, the king's near kinsman, assisted by Banquo. He has defeated the rebels under Macdonwald and slain their leader with his own hand. King Sweno, the Norwegian invader, has attacked the Scots while still in the disorder of this victory, but has been routed in his turn. The news is told in part by a wounded Sergeant, and finished by the Thane of Ross. Thus we have a complete account of Macbeth's valorous deeds, and learn of the high esteem in which he is held by the army, as well as by his fellow nobles. To this is added the King's tribute of honor to Macbeth, his brave and devoted cousin and chief general. The whole scene, then, leaves us with the highest opinion of Macbeth as a great warrior and a loyal subject. The *alarum* (or trumpet call) in the stage direction may be a sound from the conflict or quite as probably an incident of the camp. From scene 3 it appears that the King is now at or near Forres (1.3.39), and this town is nearly a hundred miles north of County Fife, where the battle is fought (line 48). However, neither Shakespeare nor his audience felt any concern about details of Scottish geography. Stage direction. **Alarum:** properly, a call to arms (*all' arme*); then, a trumpet call to the onset or to any muster. 3. **sergeant** (three syllables): an officer of much higher rank than a modern sergeant. 4. **hardy:** stout, valiant. 5. **my captivity.** Malcolm has been in the thick of the fight and would have been captured but for the Sergeant. The Prince has returned to the King's camp with a report, but he now calls upon the Sergeant for later news. The suggestion for Malcolm's adventure comes from Holinshed, where another Malcolm (one of Duncan's captains) is taken prisoner and put to death by the rebels.—**brave.** Less restricted in sense than in the modern idiom. It includes brilliant service and fine qualities in general—not merely valor. Cf. line 16.

---

†   Costume choices in this scene are critical to orienting the audience: directors have chosen to dress Duncan and his followers as warriors of the Middle Ages (reflecting the history), as nobles of the Renaissance (reflecting the time in which Shakespeare wrote), and as leaders of various wars, including World War I and II. In a play that is both history and tragedy, costume and setting are a critical signal of the prevailing ethics. [A.C.]

SERG.	Doubtful it stood,	
	As two spent swimmers that do cling together	
	And choke their art. The merciless Macdonwald	
	(Worthy to be a rebel, for to that	10
	The multiplying villanies of nature	
	Do swarm upon him) from the Western Isles	
	Of kerns and gallowglasses is supplied;	
	And Fortune, on his damned quarrel smiling,	
	Show'd like a rebel's whore. But all's too weak;	15
	For brave Macbeth (well he deserves that name),	
	Disdaining Fortune, with his brandish'd steel,	
	Which smok'd with bloody execution	
	(Like valor's minion), carv'd out his passage	
	Till he fac'd the slave;	20
	Which ne'er shook hands nor bade farewell to him	
	Till he unseam'd him from the nave to th' chaps	
	And fix'd his head upon our battlements.	
KING.	O valiant cousin! worthy gentleman!	
SERG.	As whence the sun 'gins his reflection	25
	Shipwracking storms and direful thunders break,	
	So from that spring whence comfort seem'd to come	
	Discomfort swells. Mark, King of Scotland, mark.	

8. **spent:** exhausted. 9. **choke their art:** hamper each other's movements so that neither can make use of his skill as a swimmer.—**Macdonwald:** a Scottish noble who, according to Holinshed, "tooke vpon him to be chiefe capteine of all such rebels as would stand against the king." Holinshed calls him Makdowald. 10. **to that:** as if for the very purpose (of making him a perfect rebel). To the loyal Sergeant rebellion is the worst of crimes, and it therefore seems only appropriate that Macdonwald should embody all the villainy of which human nature is capable. 12. **Western Isles:** the Hebrides. Holinshed says that "a great multitude of people" came from the Western Isles to aid Makdonwald, and adds that "no small number of Kernes and Galloglasses" from Ireland joined his army "in hope of the spoile." 13. **Of:** with.—**kerns and gallowglasses:** two kinds of Irish soldiers well known to the Elizabethans. 14. **his damned quarrel:** the accursed cause for which Macdonwald fought; "that rebellious quarell," as Holinshed calls it. The Folio reads *Quarry*. The emendation is Hanmer's. *Quarry* means "the game slaughtered in any hunt," and so is common in the sense of "prey." *His damned quarry* might mean "the loyal Scottish army, damned (condemned, doomed) in Macdonwald's mind to be his prey"; but *smiling* does not suit this interpretation, for it implies *favor*, and Fortune was not at that moment favorable to the King's men. **Show'd,** etc.: appeared to have taken Macdonwald as her lover; seemed to have granted him her favor. Fortune is often regarded as a harlot, because she shows favor to all men but is constant to none.—**all:** everything that Macdonwald and Fortune can do. 19. **minion:** darling, favorite (French *mignon*). Macdonwald appeared to be Fortune's favorite, but Macbeth was the chosen darling of Valor. 20. **slave:** villain, rascal—as a general term of abuse. 21-22. **Which...chaps:** Who was not able to part with Macbeth (to get rid of him) until Macbeth had ripped him up from the navel to the jaws. The form of expression is intentionally grotesque. *Which* refers to the *slave* (Macdonwald). 24. **cousin.** According to Holinshed, Malcolm II had two daughters; and Duncan was the son of the elder, Macbeth of the younger. This is the genealogy adopted by Shakespeare. In fact, however, Macbeth was not so nearly related to Duncan.—**worthy:** noble. 25-28. **As whence... swells:** As from the east, whence comes the sunrise, storms often break forth, so from the seeming source of comfort (the victory over Macdonwald) a disadvantage came to the Scottish army—for the King of Norway attacked them with fresh troops while still in the disorder of victory.—**gins his reflection:** begins his shining.—**spring:** source.

No sooner justice had, with valor arm'd,
Compell'd these skipping kerns to trust their heels   30
But the Norweyan lord, surveying vantage,
With furbish'd arms and new supplies of men,
Began a fresh assault.

KING.   Dismay'd not this
Our captains, Macbeth and Banquo?

SERG.   Yes,
As sparrows eagles, or the hare the lion.   35
If I say sooth, I must report they were
As cannons overcharg'd with double cracks, so they
Doubly redoubled strokes upon the foe.
Except they meant to bathe in reeking wounds,
Or memorize another Golgotha,   40
I cannot tell—
But I am faint; my gashes cry for help.

KING.   So well thy words become thee as thy wounds;
They smack of honor both. Go get him surgeons.
                                        [*Exit Sergeant, attended.*]

                    Enter Ross.

          Who comes here?

MAL.   The worthy Thane of Ross.   45

LEN.   What a haste looks through his eyes! So should he look
          That seems to speak things strange.

ROSS.   God save the King.

KING.   Whence cam'st thou, worthy thane?

ROSS.   From Fife, great King,

---

30. **skipping kerns.** *Skipping* expresses the scorn of the professional soldier for these irregular marauders, but does not necssarily imply cowardice. 31. **the Norweyan lord:** Sweno (Svend), King of Norway. In Holinshed the invasion of Scotland by Sweno is distinct from Macdonwald's rebellion, and the defeat of Sweno is followed by another invasion of Danes sent by King Canute. Shakespeare's treatment of the material is a good example of dramatic condensation.—**surveying vantage:** noting an opportune moment for attack. 34. **captains:** generals, commanders—trisyllabic, as if *capitains* (an older form of the word). 36. **sooth:** truth. 37. **cracks:** charges. Regularly used of any thunderous sound, as in iv, 1, 117: "th' crack of doom." 39. **Except:** unless. 40. **memorize...Golgotha:** make the place memorable as a second Golgotha, or field of the dead. Golgotha is Calvary. Shakespeare has adopted the explanation usual in his time, that Golgotha was so called ("the place of a skull") from the many skulls of executed persons that lay about. 41. **I cannot tell:** I do not know what their purpose was. 43. **become thee.** Duncan sees nothing unbecoming in the Sergeant's language, nor did the Elizabethan audience. He uses the style then conventionally expected of the typical soldier—a mixture of bombast and homeliness. 45. **Thane:** an old title of nobility in Scotland (Anglo-Saxon *thegn*), roughly corresponding to the English *Earl*. **seems to speak:** looks as if he were about to speak. 48. **Fife.** A county on the east coast, north of the Firth of Forth. Here Sweno was defeated, according to Holinshed. The defeat of Macdonwald took place, some time before, in Lochaber, on the other side of Scotland.

Where the Norweyan banners flout the sky
And fan our people cold. Norway himself,   50
With terrible numbers,
Assisted by that most disloyal traitor
The Thane of Cawdor, began a dismal conflict,
Till that Bellona's bridegroom, lapp'd in proof,
Confronted him with self-comparisons,   55
Point against point, rebellious arm 'gainst arm,
Curbing his lavish spirit; and to conclude,
The victory fell on us.

KING.   Great happiness!

ROSS.   That now
Sweno, the Norways' king, craves composition;
Nor would we deign him burial of his men   60
Till he disbursed, at Saint Colme's Inch,
Ten thousand dollars to our general use.

KING.   No more that Thane of Cawdor shall deceive
Our bosom interest. Go pronounce his present death
And with his former title greet Macbeth.   65

ROSS.   I'll see it done.

DUN.   What he hath lost noble Macbeth hath won.   *Exeunt.*

50-51. **Norweyan:** Norwegian.—**flout...cold:** The Norwegian banners are still flying proudly and insulting (*flouting*) the Scottish sky, as they did at the beginning of the fight, but now they serve merely to cool off our soldiers, heated by the victorious battle. The grotesque hyperbole is intentional, expressing the speaker's triumphant contempt for the vanquished foe.—**Norway:** the King of Norway. Ross takes up the story where the Sergeant dropped it. 52. Ross does not say that the Thane of Cawdor was present at the battle. There are ways of "assisting" the enemy besides fighting in his ranks. Later we learn that the help was secretly furnished. Cf. 1.3.111–114. Holinshed gives no details about Cawdor's treason and does not bring it into connection with either the rebels or Sweno. 53. **dismal:** threatening disaster (to the Scots). The original meaning of *dismal* was "ill-omened." 54. **Bellona's bridegroom.** So splendid a fighter is Macbeth that Ross speaks of Bellona, the goddess of war, as taking him for her husband. Contrast lines 16–19.—**lapp'd in proof:** wrapped (clad) in armor of proof, i.e., well-tested armor. 55. **Confronted...comparisons:** met him face to face and encountered each of his movements with one that matched it. 56. **Point...arm:** Macbeth's sword point contending against Sweno's sword point, and the rebellious arm of Sweno contending against Macbeth's arm. Sweno is not a rebel, but his arm is called *rebellious* because he is opposing the lawful monarch. Most editors shift the comma (which follows *point* in the Folios), putting it after *rebellious*; but the old punctuation makes excellent sense. 57. **lavish:** unbridled, over-confident. 58. **That:** so that. 59. **Norway's:** Norwegians'.—**craves composition:** asks for a truce, or for terms of peace. *Composition* is often used in the general sense of "agreement." 61. **Saint Colme's Inch:** St. Columba's Island; Inchcolm in the Firth of Forth. 63-64. **deceive...interest:** play me false in my most important and confidential concerns. *Our* is the so-called plural of majesty (the royal *we*).—**present:** instant.

SCENE III. [*A blasted heath.*]

Thunder. Enter the three Witches.[†]

1. WITCH.	Where hast thou been, sister?
2. WITCH.	Killing swine.
3. WITCH.	Sister, where thou?

1. WITCH.   A sailor's wife had chestnuts in her lap
And mounch'd and mounch'd and mounch'd. 'Give me,' quoth I.   5
'Aroint thee, witch!' the rump-fed ronyon cries.
Her husband's to Aleppo gone, master o' th' Tiger;
But in a sieve I'll thither sail
And, like a rat without a tail,
I'll do, I'll do, and I'll do.   10

2. WITCH.   I'll give thee a wind.

1. WITCH.   Th' art kind.

3. WITCH.   And I another.

1. WITCH.   I myself have all the other,
And the very ports they blow,   15
All the quarters that they know
I' th' shipman's card.
I will drain him dry as hay.

SCENE III.
This scene takes place before sunset (1.1.5) on the day of the battle, while Macbeth and Banquo are marching towards Forres to join the King after their double victory. The place is indicated by Macbeth's words in line 77: "this blasted heath." 2. **swine.** Witches were thought to show their malice by causing the death of domestic animals, usually by disease. Swine were often the victims, not because witches had any special enmity for them, but merely because they were a common possession, even with the poorest. 5. **mounch'd:** munched. 6. **Aroint thee:** Begone! Off with you! 129. **rump-fed:** fat-rumped.— **ronyon:** literally, scab; scabby person; but usually (as here) a mere term of abuse or contempt. 7. **th' Tiger.** A well-known name for ships in Shakespeare's time. **in a sieve.** It was believed that witches could use sieves as boats. 9. **like:** in the shape of. Witches were thought to change themselves into the forms of animals. Often, however, the animal had some defect, for the devil's creatures should not be perfect like God's. 14. **all the other:** all the others, i.e., all the other winds. By causing now this wind to blow, now that, she means to keep the Tiger tempest-tossed and far from home. 15. **ports they blow:** the harbors to which they blow. She controls the *directions* of the various winds and so can keep the Tiger away from any port. 17. **card:** compass—properly, the part of the compass on which the points are marked and over which the needle plays. 18. **drain...hay:** keep him at sea till all the water on board shall be exhausted and he shall be parched with thirst.

---

† The portrayal of the witches in film ranges from Polanski's dirty and completely realistic women to Welles' faceless and almost formless shapes. In both *Men of Respect* and *Scotland, PA*, the witches are transformed into two men and a woman. In each case, the woman is a fortune teller and the only one with magical powers. Kurosawa has only a single witch, a single figure of indeterminate age and gender, who spins ceaselessly while chanting prophecies. [A.C.]

Welles (1948) portrays the weird sisters as faceless, mysterious and not quite human.

Sleep shall neither night nor day	
Hang upon his penthouse lid.	20
He shall live a man forbid.	
Weary sev'nights, nine times nine,	
Shall he dwindle, peak, and pine.	
Though his bark cannot be lost,	
Yet it shall be tempest-tost.	25
Look what I have.	

2. WITCH. Show me! show me!

1. WITCH. Here I have a pilot's thumb,
Wrack'd as homeward he did come.   *Drum within.*

3. WITCH. A drum, a drum!   30
Macbeth doth come.

---

20. **penthouse lid.** A penthouse is a shed or lean-to attached to a building and having but one slope to its roof. The eyelid with its fringe of eyelash is compared to such a roof. 21. **forbid:** under a ban or spell. To *forbid* means, literally, "to pray *against.*" 22. **sev'-nights:** se'nnights, weeks.—**nine.** Three and its multiple nine were magic numbers. 23. **dwindle, peak, and pine.** All three verbs mean the same thing— "waste away." Cf. the old-fashioned word *peakèd* for "thin," "emaciated." 24. **cannot be lost:** since fate has decreed that it shall come safe to harbor at last. 28. **thumb.** Fragments of dead bodies were used in evil magic, and were thought to be especially powerful if the person had died a violent death. Since the pilot had been wrecked on the homeward passage, his thumb would work as a powerful charm to keep the Tiger away from port.

In contrast, Polanski's weird sisters (1971) are mundane and realistic, emphasizing human greed over supernatural power.

ALL.   The Weird Sisters, hand in hand,
               Posters of the sea and land,
               Thus do go about, about,
               Thrice to thine, and thrice to mine,   35
               And thrice again, to make up nine.
               Peace! The charm's wound up.

                         Enter Macbeth *and* Banquo.

MACB.   So foul and fair a day I have not seen.

BAN.   How far is't call'd to Forres? What are these,
               So wither'd, and so wild in their attire,   40
               That look not like th' inhabitants o' th' earth,
               And yet are on't? Live you? or are you aught
               That man may question? You seem to understand me,
               By each at once her choppy finger laying
               Upon her skinny lips. You should be women,   45

33. **Posters...land:** travellers who ride through the air, posthaste, over sea and land. 35. **Thrice to thine,** etc.: three times round (hand-in-hand in the magic dance) for thy turn, and three times for my turn. 38. The day is *foul* because of the bad weather, *fair* because of the glorious victory. Macbeth's casual remark carries our minds back to the last speech in scene 1 ("Fair is foul, and foul is fair") and thus suggests a mysterious relation, unsuspected by Macbeth himself, between him and the Weird Sisters. 43. **question:** hold converse with. 44. **choppy:** chapped. 45. **should be women:** ought to be women (to judge by your general appearance).

                    And yet your beards forbid me to interpret
                    That you are so.

MACB.   Speak, if you can. What are you?

1. WITCH.   All hail, Macbeth! Hail to thee, Thane of Glamis!

2. WITCH.   All hail, Macbeth! Hail to thee, Thane of Cawdor!

3. WITCH.   All hail, Macbeth, that shalt be King hereafter!   50

BAN.   Good sir, why do you start and seem to fear
             Things that do sound so fair? I' th' name of truth,
             Are ye fantastical, or that indeed
             Which outwardly ye show? My noble partner
             You greet with present grace and great prediction   55
             Of noble having and of royal hope,
             That he seems rapt withal. To me you speak not.
             If you can look into the seeds of time
             And say which grain will grow and which will not,
             Speak then to me, who neither beg nor fear   60
             Your favors nor your hate.

1. WITCH.   Hail!

2. WITCH.   Hail!

3. WITCH.   Hail!

1. WITCH.   Lesser than Macbeth, and greater.   65

2. WITCH.   Not so happy, yet much happier.

3. WITCH.   Thou shalt get kings, though thou be none.
             So all hail, Macbeth and Banquo!

1. WITCH.   Banquo and Macbeth, all hail!

---

46. **beards.** Witches were often thought to be bearded. 53. **fantastical:** imaginary; creatures of the deluded imagination. 54. **show:** seem, appear to be. Cf. 1.2.15. 55-56. **with...hope:** with present honor of noble possession (the two thaneships) and great prediction of royal hope (the crown). Banquo emphasizes the distinction between the mere greeting of the First and the Second Sister, on the one hand, and the actual prediction of the Third Sister, on the other. 57. **That...withal:** so that he seems carried out of himself (as in a trance) by it (your salutation). Macbeth uses almost the same words in describing his feelings in the letter to his wife (1.5): "Whiles I stood rapt in the wonder of it." 58. **seeds.** Future events are contained (in embryo) in time's seeds; their occurrence, if they come to pass, will be the sprouting of the seeds. 60-61. **neither beg...hate:** neither beg your favors nor fear your hate. 67. **get:** beget. Banquo was the mythical ancestor of the royal Stuarts.

Macb.	Stay, you imperfect speakers, tell me more!	70
	By Sinel's death I know I am Thane of Glamis;	
	But how of Cawdor? The Thane of Cawdor lives,	
	A prosperous gentleman; and to be King	
	Stands not within the prospect of belief,	
	No more than to be Cawdor. Say from whence	75
	You owe this strange intelligence, or why	
	Upon this blasted heath you stop our way	
	With such prophetic greeting. Speak, I charge you.	

Witches vanish.†

Ban.	The earth hath bubbles, as the water has,	
	And these are of them. Whither are they vanish'd?	80
Macb.	Into the air, and what seem'd corporal melted	
	As breath into the wind. Would they had stay'd.	
Ban.	Were such things here as we do speak about?	
	Or have we eaten on the insane root	
	That takes the reason prisoner?	85
Macb.	Your children shall be kings.	
Ban.	You shall be King.	
Macb.	And Thane of Cawdor too. Went it not so?	
Ban.	To th' selfsame tune and words. Who's here?	

Enter Ross *and* Angus.

---

71. Macbeth's father Finlaeg (Finlay), Thane of Glamis, had died shortly before. Holinshed (following Boece and Bellenden) calls him *Sinell*. 74. **the prospect of belief:** the farthest look into the future that belief can take. 75-76. **from whence...intelligence:** from what source you have this strange information. Manifestly the prophesy is supernatural: is it derived from good spirits or from demons? Macbeth balances the same question in lines 130–137.—**owe:** own, possess, have. 80. **are of them:** belong to that category. 81. **corporal:** corporeal, material. 84. **the insane root:** probably hemlock root (one of the ingredients in the hell-broth in 4.1.25), though other roots were known to have a similar effect.—**insane:** causing insanity.

---

† It is unclear if Shakespeare originally intended his witches to "vanish" through trapdoors or fly off stage on wires. In the 17th century, D'Avenant began a tradition of the witches flying on and off stage, which continued until Garrick, in the 19th century, had them rise and sink through trapdoors. Film, of course, allows for them to literally vanish, which makes it more noticeable when they do not, as in Polanski's version, where they simply run away, making Macbeth's claim that they have vanished a lie. In Welles' version, they are driven off by the appearance of the Holy Father, a creation of Welles. [A.C.]

ROSS.   The King hath happily receiv'd, Macbeth,
                     The news of thy success; and when he reads   90
                     Thy personal venture in the rebels' fight,
                     His wonders and his praises do contend
                     Which should be thine or his. Silenc'd with that,
                     In viewing o'er the rest o' th' selfsame day,
                     He finds thee in the stout Norweyan ranks,   95
                     Nothing afeard of what thyself didst make,
                     Strange images of death. As thick as hail
                     Came post with post, and every one did bear
                     Thy praises in his kingdom's great defense
                     And pour'd them down before him.

ANG.   We are sent   100
                     To give thee from our royal master thanks;
                     Only to herald thee into his sight,
                     Not pay thee.

ROSS.   And for an earnest of a greater honor,
                     He bade me, from him, call thee Thane of Cawdor;   105
                     In which addition, hail, most worthy Thane!
                     For it is thine.

BAN.   What, can the devil speak true?

MACB.   The Thane of Cawdor lives. Why do you dress me
                     In borrowed robes?

ANG.   Who was the Thane lives yet,
                     But under heavy judgment bears that life   110
                     Which he deserves to lose. Whether he was combin'd
                     With those of Norway, or did line the rebel
                     With hidden help and vantage, or that with both

---

89–97. Ross refers particularly to both parts of the double victory, as the Sergeant had done (1.2)—
to the battle with the rebels (including the single combat with Macdonwald) and to the defeat of
the Norwegian king. 92-93. **His wonders...his:** The wonder he feels (which tends to make him
speechless—dumb with admiration) vies with the wish he has to utter thy praises. If the wonder
remains *his* (i.e., if he continues to feel it to its full extent), he will be unable to speak, and therefore the
praises (being unuttered) will not be *thine*. On the other hand, if the praises win the day and insist on
being uttered, then he will no longer be *dumb* with wonder. The result of the contention is *silence* on
the King's part: his wonder wins the contest.—**with that:** by that contest between dumb wonder and
the wish to utter praise. 96. **Nothing afeard:** not at all afraid. 97. **Strange images of death:** death in
strange and dreadful forms. Ross suggests that it is natural for so great a warrior as Macbeth to feel
no fear of suffering death when he was so fully occupied in inflicting it on the foe.98. **post with post:**
one messenger riding post after another. 104. **earnest:** a small payment in advance to bind a bargain;
hence, a specimen and assurance of what is to come. 106. **addition:** title. Ross unwittingly repeats the
salutation of the Second Sister.—**worthy:** noble. Cf. 1.2.24. 111. **combin'd:** secretly allied. 112. **line
the rebel:** support Macdonwald. 113. **hidden help.** Clearly he was not present and fighting in the
battle. Macbeth knew nothing about his treason. Cf. note on 1.2.52.—**vantage:** opportunity.—**both:**
i.e., both the rebel Macdonwald and the king of Norway.

He labor'd in his country's wrack, I know not;
But treasons capital, confess'd and prov'd,   115
Have overthrown him.

MACB.   [aside]   Glamis, and Thane of Cawdor!
The greatest is behind.—[To Ross and Angus.] Thanks for your pains.
[Aside to Banquo] Do you not hope your children shall be kings,
When those that gave the Thane of Cawdor to me
Promis'd no less to them?

BAN.   [aside to Macbeth]   That, trusted home,   120
Might yet enkindle you unto the crown,
Besides the Thane of Cawdor. But 'tis strange.
And oftentimes, to win us to our harm,
The instruments of darkness tell us truths,
Win us with honest trifles, to betray's   125
In deepest consequence.—
Cousins, a word, I pray you.

MACB.   [aside]   Two truths are told,
As happy prologues to the swelling act
Of the imperial theme.—I thank you, gentlemen.—
[Aside] This supernatural soliciting   130
Cannot be ill; cannot be good. If ill,
Why hath it given me earnest of success,
Commencing in a truth? I am Thane of Cawdor.
If good, why do I yield to that suggestion
Whose horrid image doth unfix my hair   135
And make my seated heart knock at my ribs
Against the use of nature? Present fears
Are less than horrible imaginings.
My thought, whose murder yet is but fantastical,

---

117. **is behind:** remains, to follow in due succession. 120. **home:** to the full; to its logical conclusion. 125-126. **Win us:** gain our confidence.—**betray's...consequence:** disappoint our hopes in something of great importance that was to follow. 127. **Cousins.** A common greeting among noblemen, most of whom were in fact related on account of frequent intermarriages. Banquo steps aside to converse with Ross and Angus, and thus an opportunity is given for Macbeth's soliloquy. 128. **swelling:** stately. 130. **soliciting:** attempt to influence me. 132. **earnest of success:** an assurance or pledge of what is to follow (that is, of the promised kingship). Cf. line 104. *Success* does not mean "prosperity in my efforts," but merely "what is to follow," "the future." The fulfilment of the prophecy about the thaneship of Cawdor is the *earnest*, since it shows that the Weird Sisters tell the truth. Macbeth argues that, since Satan is the father of lies (cf. line 107), a truthful prophecy can hardly be of diabolical origin. 134. **yield to:** give access to, allow it to enter my mind.—**suggestion:** evil thought, temptation. 136. **seated:** firm and intrepid; not easily agitated. 137. **Against the use of nature:** contrary to my natural habit (for Macbeth is not accustomed to feel fear).—**Present fears:** actual objects of fear; frightful things that are before one's eyes. Cf. lines 95–97. 139. **fantastical:** imaginary. Cf. line 53.

	Shakes so my single state of man that function 140
	Is smother'd in surmise and nothing is
	But what is not.
BAN.	Look how our partner's rapt.
MACB.	[*aside*] If chance will have me King, why, chance may crown me,
	Without my stir.
BAN.	New honors come upon him,
	Like our strange garments, cleave not to their mould 145
	But with the aid of use.
MACB.	[*aside*] Come what come may,
	Time and the hour runs through the roughest day.
BAN.	Worthy Macbeth, we stay upon your leisure.
MACB.	Give me your favor. My dull brain was wrought
	With things forgotten. Kind gentlemen, your pains 150
	Are regist'red where every day I turn
	The leaf to read them. Let us toward the King.
	[*Aside to Banquo*] Think upon what hath chanc'd; and, at more time,
	The interim having weigh'd it, let us speak
	Our free hearts each to other.
BAN.	[*aside to Macbeth*] Very gladly. 155
MACB.	[*aside to Banquo*] Till then, enough.—
	Come, friends. *Exeunt.*

---

140. **my single state of man:** my weak human condition; my nature as a poor, feeble human creature. 140-141. **function...not:** all my senses and faculties (my powers of mind and body) are absorbed and brought into a state of trance by my vision of a future deed (the murder of Duncan), so that I am unconscious of my actual surroundings in the present, and see and feel only the unreal future. 142. **Look...rapt.** Banquo and his friends have finished their private conference and observe the abstraction of Macbeth.—**rapt.** Cf. line 57. 145. **cleave...mould:** do not fit or adapt themselves comfortably to the wearer's form. 146. **use:** habit, custom. 147. **Time...day:** Time, advancing steadily hour by hour, brings even the roughest day to an end.—**stay upon your leisure:** await your convenience. 149. **Give...favor:** Pardon me.—**wrought:** disturbed, agitated. Macbeth courteously excuses his fit of abstraction as due to his suddenly remembering important business that had slipped his mind. 151. **regist'red:** i.e., "within the book and volume of my brain" (*Hamlet*, 1.5). 152. **Let us toward the King.** The omission of a verb of motion is a common Elizabethan idiom. 153. **at more time:** when we have more leisure. 154. **The interim...it:** when we have thought it over in the meantime. The *interim* or *interval* is personified, and is represented as itself considering the matter. 155. **Our free hearts:** our thoughts and feelings freely.

SCENE IV. [*Forres. The Palace.*]†

Flourish. Enter King [Duncan], Lennox, Malcolm, Donalbain, *and* Attendants.

KING. Is execution done on Cawdor? Are not
   Those in commission yet return'd?

MAL.   My liege,
   They are not yet come back. But I have spoke
   With one that saw him die; who did report
   That very frankly he confess'd his treasons,   5
   Implor'd your Highness' pardon, and set forth
   A deep repentance. Nothing in his life
   Became him like the leaving it. He died
   As one that had been studied in his death
   To throw away the dearest thing he ow'd   10
   As 'twere a careless trifle.

KING.   There's no art
   To find the mind's construction in the face.
   He was a gentleman on whom I built
   An absolute trust.

     Enter Macbeth, Banquo, Ross, *and* Angus.
       O worthiest cousin,
   The sin of my ingratitude even now   15
   Was heavy on me! Thou art so far before
   That swiftest wing of recompense is slow
   To overtake thee. Would thou hadst less deserv'd,
   That the proportion both of thanks and payment

SCENE IV.
This scene takes place on the day after the events of scenes 1–3. In the meantime Ross has dispatched the commissioners with the King's order for the execution of Cawdor (lines 64–66), and the report of his penitence and death has reached Malcolm's ears. 2. **Those in commission:** the royal commissioners appointed to attend to Cawdor's trial and execution. 9-11. **had been...trifle:** had learned the lesson how, at death, to part with his dearest possession (life) easily.—**ow'd:** owned.—**As:** as if.—**careless:** uncared-for, worthless, insignificant. 12. **construction:** interpretation. Duncan has barely uttered these words when another trusted vassal enters, whose face also he has no art to construe. 16. Duncan uses the familiar and affectionate *thou* instead of the more formal *you* in speaking to his near kinsman. 19. **the proportion:** the larger proportion; the preponderance.

---

† Welles chose to stage Cawdor's execution, intercutting it with shots of Macbeth racing home and greeting his wife–as Cawdor is hanged, Macbeth and Lady Macbeth kiss with intense passion. [A.C.]

Might have been mine! Only I have left to say,   20
More is thy due than more than all can pay.

MACB.   The service and the loyalty I owe,
In doing it pays itself. Your Highness' part
Is to receive our duties; and our duties
Are to your throne and state children and servants,   25
Which do but what they should by doing everything
Safe toward your love and honor.

KING.   Welcome hither.
I have begun to plant thee and will labor
To make thee full of growing. Noble Banquo,
That hast no less deserv'd, nor must be known   30
No less to have done so, let me infold thee
And hold thee to my heart.

BAN.   There if I grow,
The harvest is your own.

KING.   My plenteous joys,
Wanton in fullness, seek to hide themselves
In drops of sorrow. Sons, kinsmen, thanes,   35
And you whose places are the nearest, know
We will establish our estate upon
Our eldest, Malcolm, whom we name hereafter
The Prince of Cumberland; which honor must
Not unaccompanied invest him only,   40
But signs of nobleness, like stars, shall shine

---

20. **mine** (emphatic): on *my* side of the account—so that the balance might stand in my favor (as having paid more than I owed). 21. **More...pay:** And so, even if I should give thee all I possess, the balance would still stand against me. 23. **pays itself:** is its own recompense. 24-27. **our duties...everything:** Our duties are in the same situation with reference to your throne and royal position (*state*) in which children are with reference to their parents and servants with reference to their masters; for, like children and servants, we can do no more than we ought, no matter how much we may do.—**everything... honor:** everything that tends to safeguard and fulfil our obligation to love and honor you. 28. **to plant thee:** i.e., by making thee Thane of Cawdor. 32. **grow.** Banquo speaks in his accustomed half-jesting vein, echoing the word *grow* just used by the King: "If I take root when you press me to your heart, and grow there like a tree, whatever fruit I bear shall be yours." 34. **Wanton:** perverse, contrary, since tears are the natural expression rather of sorrow than of joy. 37-38. **We will:** it is our royal purpose. Duncan changes from the singular *I* to the royal *we*.—**establish...Malcolm:** settle my royal rank upon Malcolm as my recognized successor. 39. **Prince of Cumberland.** The throne of Scotland was elective within the limits of the royal family. When Duncan died, the electors were not unlikely to prefer Macbeth, Duncan's cousin, to a young and inexperienced prince like Malcolm. But Duncan's expressed purpose of making Malcolm Prince of Cumberland would, if it were carried out, involve his recognition as heir apparent by all the nobility, and they would thus pledge themselves to elect him when his father should die. It is the "irony of fate" that Duncan takes occasion to signalize his joy over Macbeth's victories by nominating Malcolm Prince of Cumberland, thus signing his own death warrant. 41. There is to be a general distribution of honors when the Prince is formally invested with his new title.

	On all deservers. From hence to Inverness,	
	And bind us further to you.	
MACB.	The rest is labor, which is not us'd for you.	
	I'll be myself the harbinger, and make joyful	45
	The hearing of my wife with your approach;	
	So, humbly take my leave.	
KING.	My worthy Cawdor.	
MACB.	[aside] The Prince of Cumberland! That is a step	
	On which I must fall down, or else o'erleap,	
	For in my way it lies. Stars, hide your fires!	50
	Let not light see my black and deep desires.	
	The eye wink at the hand, yet let that be,	
	Which the eye fears, when it is done, to see. *Exit.*	
KING.	True, worthy Banquo: he is full so valiant,	
	And in his commendations I am fed;	55
	It is a banquet to me. Let's after him,	
	Whose care is gone before to bid us welcome.	
	It is a peerless kinsman. *Flourish.*	
	Exeunt.	

SCENE V. [*Inverness.* Macbeth's *Castle.*]

Enter Macbeth's Wife,† *alone, with a letter.*

LADY.	[*reads*] "They met me in the day of success; and I have learn'd by the
	perfect'st report they have more in them than mortal knowledge. When

---

42. **Inverness:** where Macbeth's castle is. 43. **bind...you:** oblige me still further by receiving me as a guest. 44. **The rest...you:** Even repose, when not used in your service, ceases to be rest and becomes toil. Hence Macbeth will not tarry, but will hasten home to prepare for Duncan's visit. 45. **harbinger:** an officer sent ahead (when a king intends to visit a place) to arrange for proper lodgings (*harbourage*) for him and his suite. 48. **a step:** an advance in honor (for Malcolm). 49. **fall down...o'erleap:** i.e., if Malcolm is Prince of Cumberland I must either give up all hope of kingship, or must win the crown by my own efforts, in spite of his being the acknowledged successor. 52. **The eye wink at the hand:** Let my eyes not see the deed that my hand commits. 58. **It:** common in the familiar style to express affection, as here, or contempt.

SCENE V.
This scene takes place on the same day as scene 4,—the second day of the action. Lady Macbeth reads only the last part of the letter aloud. What she omits contained matters with which we are already familiar—an account of the battle, of the meeting with the Weird Sisters, of their greeting and prophecy. The letter was written and dispatched in the interval between scene 3 and scene 4, before Duncan had invited himself to Macbeth's castle. 1. **in the day of success:** on my lucky day (the day on which I had won the battle), so that I may put greater faith in their prophecy.

---

† In Kurosawa, Lady Asaji is almost inhumanly still, moving only with a terrible slowness. Polanski, on the other hand, created a delicate Lady Macbeth in Francesca Annis, who, right from the start, is overwhelmed by what is being offered. [A.C.]

I burn'd in desire to question them further, they made themselves air,
into which they vanish'd. Whiles I stood rapt in the wonder of it, came
missives from the King, who all-hail'd me Thane of Cawdor, by which
title, before, these Weird Sisters saluted me, and referr'd me to the
coming on of time with 'Hail, King that shalt be!' This have I thought
good to deliver thee, my dearest partner of greatness, that thou mightst
not lose the dues of rejoicing by being ignorant of what greatness is
promis'd thee. Lay it to thy heart, and farewell."   10

Glamis thou art, and Cawdor, and shalt be—
What thou art promis'd. Yet do I fear thy nature.
It is too full o' th' milk of human kindness
To catch the nearest way. Thou wouldst be great;
Art not without ambition, but without   15
The illness should attend it. What thou wouldst highly,
That wouldst thou holily; wouldst not play false,
And yet wouldst wrongly win. Thou'ldst have, great Glamis,
That which cries "Thus thou must do," if thou have it;
And that which rather thou dost fear to do   20
Than wishest should be undone. Hie thee hither,
That I may pour my spirits in thine ear
And chastise with the valor of my tongue
All that impedes thee from the golden round
Which fate and metaphysical aid doth seem   25
To have thee crown'd withal.

Enter Messenger.

---

4. **Whiles:** while.—**I stood rapt.** Once more a repetition of the language of the third scene: "Look
how our partner's rapt" (1.3.142). 5. **missives:** messengers. 8. **deliver thee:** report to thee.—**partner
of greatness.** Macbeth and his wife are so deeply attached to each other that neither can think of any
division or individuality in their interests. Cf. lines 55–59, 70, 71. 13. **th' milk of human kindness.**
Milk is often used metaphorically for the kindly and gentle qualities in human nature (line 44). Cf.
4.3.98: "the sweet milk of concord." 14. **the nearest way.** Like Macbeth, she thinks at once of murder
as the nearest way. Unlike him, however, she does not try to banish the thought, but entertains it as
a definite purpose in which she never falters. This is characteristic of Lady Macbeth: her mind works
with directness and intense simplicity, and her will is of steel. The nearest way becomes, in the lines
that follow, the only way, for she has no patience with any but the shortest route to any destination. 16.
The illness should attend it: the evil quality (ruthlessness) which should always accompany ambition.
18. **wouldst wrongly win:** You are like a gambler who is unwilling to cheat, and yet is eager to win a
stake that cannot be won without false play. 19–21. The cry is merely *"Thus* thou must do." The rest of
the sentence is Lady Macbeth's own comment: "You wish to have the crown; and the crown, if you're
to have it at all, demands of you one particular deed: it cries '*Thus* thou must do!' And your reluctance
so to act comes rather from a weak fear of sinning than from any strong wish that the deed should not
be done. You would not mourn for the King if he were to be killed by accident, or by some third party,
without any guilt of yours." 22. **my spirits:** my resolution and energy of will. 23. **chástise:** rebuke and
suppress. 24. **All that impedes thee:** i.e., gentleness of nature and scruples of conscience.—**golden
round.** Cf. 4.1.88–89: "the round And top of sovereignty." 25-26. **metaphysical:** supernatural.—
seem...withal: seem to intend to cause thee to be crowned with. *Withal* means simply "with," as often
at the end of a phrase.

What is your tidings?

MESS.   The King comes here tonight.

LADY.   Thou'rt mad to say it!
Is not thy master with him? who, were't so,
Would have inform'd for preparation.

MESS.   So please you, it is true. Our Thane is coming.   30
One of my fellows had the speed of him,
Who, almost dead for breath, had scarcely more
Than would make up his message.

LADY.   Give him tending;
He brings great news.   *Exit Messenger.*
                   The raven himself is hoarse
That croaks the fatal entrance of Duncan   35
Under my battlements. Come, you spirits
That tend on mortal thoughts, unsex me here,
And fill me, from the crown to the toe, top-full
Of direst cruelty. Make thick my blood;
Stop up th' access and passage to remorse,   40
That no compunctious visitings of nature
Shake my fell purpose nor keep peace between
Th' effect and it. Come to my woman's breasts
And take my milk for gall, you murth'ring ministers,
Wherever in your sightless substances   45
You wait on nature's mischief. Come, thick night,
And pall thee in the dunnest smoke of hell,
That my keen knife see not the wound it makes,

---

27. **Thou'rt mad to say it!** To the messenger this sounds merely like a strong expression of surprise, but the audience understands the excitement with which the Lady greets what seems to her like "fate and metaphysical aid." So in line 34 "great news" means one thing to the innocent messenger, another to the audience. 29. **inform'd:** sent me information of the visit. 31. **had the speed of:** outstripped. 34. **The raven.** There are ravens flying about the castle, and their croak, now heard by Lady Macbeth, seems to her even hoarser than usual, as if they were predicting the King's death. 35. **entrance:** *Fatal* has a double meaning— "directed by fate" and "fatal to Duncan." 36. **you spirits.** A direct invocation to those evil spirits, whatever they may be, that are always ready to foster murderous thoughts— "the instruments of darkness," as Banquo calls them in 1.3.124. 37. **mortal:** deadly, murderous. 39. **Make thick my blood.** Blood thickened by melancholy was thought to cause gloomy ferocity of disposition. 45. **th' accéss... remorse:** every way of approach by which compassion can come to my heart. 41. **compunctious...nature:** natural instincts of compassion. 42. **fell:** cruel, savage. 42-43. **keep peace...it:** come between my cruel purpose and its fulfilment (*effect*), so as to prevent that fulfilment and thus to keep the peace. 49. **for:** in exchange for. Take away milk (which signifies gentleness: see line 18) and substitute gall (which signifies bitter resentment or enmity). The *murth'ring ministers* (i.e., agents, assistants) are the "spirits that tend on mortal thoughts." 45. **sightless:** invisible. 46. **wait on...mischief:** are on the watch to help forward any of the evil deeds to which our nature is prone. 47. **pall:** cover as with a pall or mantle, enshroud.—**dunnest:** darkest. Cf. 2.4.5–11. 48. **my keen knife.** Lady Macbeth so identifies herself with her husband's acts that she thinks of the deed as her own (cf. 2.2.13–14).

Nor heaven peep through the blanket of the dark
To cry "Hold, hold!"

Enter Macbeth

Great Glamis! worthy Cawdor!   50
Greater than both, by the all-hail hereafter!
Thy letters have transported me beyond
This ignorant present, and I feel now
The future in the instant.

MACB.   My dearest love,
Duncan comes here tonight.

LADY.   And when goes hence?   55

MACB.   Tomorrow, as he purposes.

LADY.   O, never
Shall sun that morrow see.
Your face, my Thane, is as a book where men
May read strange matters. To beguile the time,
Look like the time; bear welcome in your eye,   60
Your hand, your tongue; look like the innocent flower,
But be the serpent under't. He that's coming
Must be provided for; and you shall put
This night's great business into my dispatch,
Which shall to all our nights and days to come   65
Give solely sovereign sway and masterdom.

MACB.   We will speak further.

LADY.   Only look up clear.
To alter favor ever is to fear.
Leave all the rest to me.   *Exeunt.*

---

49. **peep:** as with the eye of one single star. 52-53. **transported me:** swept me forward as in a vision.—
ignorant. The present is *ignorant* because the substantial fulfilment of one's hopes and fears is known only
to the future. 54. **the instant:** the present moment. 64. **great business.** Lady Macbeth, whose eye is on
the object to be attained, thinks and speaks of the murder as a glorious deed. The splendor of the prize
is reflected in her mind on the action itself.—**dispatch:** management. 67. **We will speak further.** In
this further conference on the subject, which must be imagined to take place between this scene and the
next (before Duncan's arrival), Macbeth declares his resolution to kill the King. Lady Macbeth repeats
the upshot of it in 1.7.47–59.—**clear:** with an unruffled countenance. Cf. 3.2.27–28: "Gentle my lord,
sleek o'er your rugged looks, Be bright and jovial among your guests to-night." 68. **To alter...fear:**
When a person shows a disturbed countenance, it is always inferred that he has something on his
mind—and that may rouse suspicion among our guests.—**favor:** countenance, expression.

SCENE VI. [*Inverness. Before* Macbeth's *castle.*]

Hautboys and torches. Enter King [Duncan], Malcolm, Donalbain, Banquo,
Lennox, Macduff, Ross, Angus, *and* Attendants.

KING.   This castle hath a pleasant seat. The air
            Nimbly and sweetly recommends itself
            Unto our gentle senses.

BAN.   This guest of summer,
            The temple-haunting martlet, does approve
            By his lov'd mansionry that the heaven's breath   5
            Smells wooingly here. No jutty, frieze,
            Buttress, nor coign of vantage, but this bird
            Hath made his pendent bed and procreant cradle.
            Where they most breed and haunt, I have observ'd
            The air is delicate.

Enter Lady [Macbeth].

KING.   See, see, our honor'd hostess!   10
            The love that follows us sometime is our trouble,
            Which still we thank as love. Herein I teach you
            How you shall bid God 'ield us for your pains
            And thank us for your trouble.

LADY.   All our service
            In every point twice done, and then done double,   15
            Were poor and single business to contend
            Against those honors deep and broad wherewith
            Your Majesty loads our house. For those of old,

SCENE VI.
This scene takes place toward night on the same day as scene 5 (see 1.5.60). The horror of the situation
is only increased by the cheerful confidence which Duncan shows in approaching the place of slaughter.
1. **seat:** situation, site. 2, 3. **The air...senses:** The air, by its freshness and sweetness, appeals pleasantly
to our senses and makes them gentle—i.e., soothes them. 4. **martlet:** the house martin, [a bird] called
"temple-haunting" because it often builds about churches.—**approve:** prove. 5. **By...mansionry:** by the
fact that he has chosen this as a favorite site for his mansions. 6. **wooingly:** so as to appeal to the senses
by its delightful freshness.—**jutty:** out-jutting place in the building. 7. **coign of vantage:** advantageous
corner or angle. 8. **procreant cradle:** "cradle where he breeds" (Davenant). 11–14. Duncan begins
with a general statement: "We sometimes find that the love which others feel for us actually gives us
trouble, because they follow us about and force their attentions on us; yet we always (*still*) are grateful
for such affection, because it is *love,* of which one cannot have too much." Then he makes a particular
application of this principle to the present circumstances. "Herein (i.e., in making this remark) I am
teaching you, Lady Macbeth, how to pray God to reward me for the efforts I am causing you to make in
receiving me as your guest, and also how to thank me for the trouble I am giving you by my visit—for
the visit is due to my love for you and your husband."—**'ield:** yield, i.e., repay. 16, 17. **single:** feeble,
insignificant—here in special antithesis to *double.*—**contend against:** vie with, offset.

And the late dignities heap'd up to them,
We rest your hermits.

KING.   Where's the Thane of Cawdor?   20
We cours'd him at the heels and had a purpose
To be his purveyor; but he rides well,
And his great love, sharp as his spur, hath holp him
To his home before us. Fair and noble hostess,
We are your guest tonight.

LADY.   Your servants ever   25
Have theirs, themselves, and what is theirs, in compt,
To make their audit at your Highness' pleasure,
Still to return your own.

KING.   Give me your hand;
Conduct me to mine host. We love him highly
And shall continue our graces towards him.   30
By your leave, hostess.   *Exeunt.*

---

19. **late dignities:** the thaneships of Glamis and Cawdor. 20. **We rest your hermits:** we remain your grateful beadsmen. 21. **We:** plural for *I* (the "royal *we*").—**cours'd him:** rode rapidly after him. 22. **púrveyor:** literally, an officer who precedes a king or a great noble when on a journey and makes arrangements for provisions and other supplies. See note on 1.4.45: "I'll be myself the harbinger." 23. **holp:** old form for *helped*. 26. **theirs:** their vassals and dependents.—**what is theirs:** all their possessions.—**in compt:** on account, on deposit (not as their own property, but as something entrusted to them by you). 27. **make their audit:** render their account (as an agent or banker must do). 28. **Still:** always, at any moment. She means that everything she and her husband have is really the King's, and that he has the right to call for it, or any part of it, at any time. 30. **graces:** royal favors.

Scene VII. [*Inverness.* Macbeth's *Castle.*]

Hautboys. Torches. Enter a Sewer, *and divers* Servants
with dishes and service over the stage.

Then enter Macbeth.

Macb.	If it were done when 'tis done, then 'twere well	
	It were done quickly. If th' assassination	
	Could trammel up the consequence, and catch,	
	With his surcease, success; that but this blow	
	Might be the be-all and the end-all here,	5
	But here, upon this bank and shoal of time,	
	We'ld jump the life to come. But in these cases	
	We still have judgment here, that we but teach	
	Bloody instructions, which, being taught, return	
	To plague th' inventor. This even-handed justice	10
	Commends th' ingredient of our poison'd chalice	
	To our own lips. He's here in double trust:	
	First, as I am his kinsman and his subject—	
	Strong both against the deed; then, as his host,	
	Who should against his murderer shut the door,	15
	Not bear the knife myself. Besides, this Duncan	

Scene VII.

This scene takes place on the same day as scenes 4–6. Supper is in progress in the great hall of Macbeth's castle at Inverness. The Sewer is the butler who has charge of serving the supper; *service* means "viands," "a course." 1–24. The three dissuading reasons form a climax. The lowest stands first—mere prudence; then, on a higher plane, comes loyalty, in its threefold aspect of kinship, allegiance, and hospitality; and finally, most powerful of all, there is "human kindness": to murder so gracious a king will be horrible; the whole world will be overcome with pity for the victim. In short, to kill Duncan would be unwise, disloyal, and monstrously cruel. I can find no incitement, then, but reckless ambition—and unrestrained ambition ruins itself. The upshot of the matter is expressed in line 31: "We will proceed no further in this business." It is characteristic of Macbeth's nature (as described by his wife in 1.5.18) that pity comes at the acme of the climax. 1-2. **If it were done when 'tis done,** etc. The first *done* and *'tis* are both emphatic: If the whole business were *over and done with* as soon as the mere deed had been done, then it would be well to act without delay. The next sentence repeats the same thought in outspoken terms and full detail. 3. **Could...consequence:** could catch as in a trammel (a net used to catch birds or fish [A.C.]) that which may follow (and so prevent its occurrence). 4. **his surcease:** Duncan's death; his ceasing to exist.—**success:** the future (as in 1.3.132)—not (as in modern usage) a successful outcome. Macbeth, dwelling on the thought, expresses it twice in almost identical terms; for "catch success" is synonymous with "trammel up the consequence." Many scholars take *his* in the sense of *its* and interpret *his surcease* as "the surcease of the consequence"; but this is harder and less likely.—**that:** so that. 5. **the be-all and the end-all:** all there is to the matter, and the end of the whole affair. 6. **But here:** only *here,* i.e., in this world only.—**bank and shoal of time.** A man's lifetime is a mere sandbank or bar, soon to be covered by the sea of eternity. 7. **jump the life to come:** risk eternity; take a leap in the dark so far as the next world is concerned. 8-10. **still:** always.—**here:** in this world.—**that...inventor:** so that he who murders a king in order to get the crown is teaching others how to murder *him* for the same purpose. 11. **Commends:** puts, applies.—**th' ingredient** (collective): the elements composing the draught in the chalice.

Hath borne his faculties so meek, hath been
So clear in his great office, that his virtues
Will plead like angels, trumpet-tongu'd, against
The deep damnation of his taking-off;   20
And pity, like a naked new-born babe,
Striding the blast, or heaven's cherubin, hors'd
Upon the sightless couriers of the air,
Shall blow the horrid deed in every eye,
That tears shall drown the wind. I have no spur   25
To prick the sides of my intent, but only
Vaulting ambition, which o'erleaps itself
And falls on th' other side.

Enter Lady [Macbeth].

How now? What news?

LADY.   He has almost supp'd. Why have you left the chamber?

MACB.   Hath he ask'd for me?

LADY.   Know you not he has?   30

MACB.   We will proceed no further in this business.
He hath honor'd me of late, and I have bought
Golden opinions from all sorts of people,
Which would be worn now in their newest gloss,
Not cast aside so soon.

LADY.   Was the hope drunk   35
Wherein you dress'd yourself? Hath it slept since?
And wakes it now to look so green and pale
At what it did so freely? From this time
Such I account thy love. Art thou afeard

---

17. **borne...meek:** exercised his powers and privileges with so mild a sway. 18. **clear:** free from blame; void of reproach. 21. **babe.** Such an infant is a fit object for human tenderness and therefore an apt emblem for Compassion. Or Pity (as Macbeth's imagination, roused to full activity by his emotions, conceives) may take the form of an angelic messenger (*cherubin*) sent from heaven to spread the tidings.—**Striding the blast:** riding the wind—because the feeling of compassion will spread through the realm as if borne "on the wings of all the winds." Cf. *Psalms*, xviii, 10. 23. **sightless:** invisible (1.5.50).—**couriers:** coursers, steeds. 25. **That:** so that.—**drown the wind:** as heavy rain is said to do. 25-28. Ambition, first thought of as a *spur*, becomes the horseman who, meaning to vault into the saddle, springs too high and falls disgracefully. 29. **supp'd:** finished supper.—**chamber:** the dining room, hall. 33. **all sorts of people.** In 1.2, Shakespeare has taken pains to show how high Macbeth stands with "all sorts of people" from the Sergeant, who expresses the feelings of the army, to the highest nobility and the King himself. The present speech proves the deliberate expository purpose of that scene. 34. **would be:** wish to be, demand to be—and so practically equivalent to "ought to be" or "must be." 35-37. **Was the hope,** etc.: Was the hope that you expressed to me a little while ago like a reveler, who wakes next morning sallow of face and is nauseated by the mere thought of his last night's debauch?—**dress'd.** Macbeth has just used such a figure, and his wife picks it up and gives it a scornful turn. 39. **Such:** just as fickle as your resolution has proved.

	To be the same in thine own act and valor	40

To be the same in thine own act and valor   40
As thou art in desire? Wouldst thou have that
Which thou esteem'st the ornament of life,
And live a coward in thine own esteem,
Letting "I dare not" wait upon "I would,"
Like the poor cat i' th' adage?

MACB.   Prithee peace!   45
I dare do all that may become a man.
Who dares do more is none.

LADY.   What beast was't then
That made you break this enterprise to me?
When you durst do it, then you were a man;
And to be more than what you were, you would   50
Be so much more the man. Nor time nor place
Did then adhere, and yet you would make both.
They have made themselves, and that their fitness now
Does unmake you. I have given suck, and know
How tender 'tis to love the babe that milks me.[†]   55
I would, while it was smiling in my face,
Have pluck'd my nipple from his boneless gums
And dash'd the brains out, had I so sworn as you
Have done to this.

MACB.   If we should fail?

LADY.   We fail?

---

42. **the ornament of life:** life's chief adornment—the crown. 43. **And live a coward:** i.e., do without it, and always accuse yourself of cowardice when you think of the opportunity you have lost.—**esteem:** opinion. 44. **wait upon:** constantly attend, always follow. 45. An adage or proverb, "the cat would eat fish, but would not wet her feet," indicating a desire for success without the willingness to suffer discomfort [A.C.]. 50-52. **And to be...man:** And by being more daring than you were then—by daring to *do* what you then dared to *resolve*—you would be even more the man than you then were.—**Nor... both:** When we had that conversation, Duncan (though expected) was not at our castle. Neither time nor place, therefore, was consistent with action at that moment. Yet you were quite ready to *make* an opportunity in case he should not come after all. You were brave enough when there was no chance to act. Now that the moment has come, its presence unmans you. 53. **have made themselves:** i.e., by Duncan's visit, which puts him in our power.—**that their fitness:** that very fitness of time and place. 54. **unmake:** unnerve, unman. 59. **We fail?** Since all Lady Macbeth's speeches in this dialogue begin with a scornful question, this is best taken in the same way, as an exclamatory question indicating impossibility, not merely as a statement ("If we fail, we fail").

---

† Both Kurosawa and Reilly literalize this speech: Lady Asaji becomes pregnant and miscarries, driving her to madness, while Ruthie uses her husband's insistence that she have an abortion as motivation. [A.C.]

Lady Macbeth cradles Macbeth like a child, demonstrating that she is the stronger of the two (Polanski, 1971).

But screw your courage to the sticking place,   60
And we'll not fail. When Duncan is asleep
(Whereto the rather shall his day's hard journey
Soundly invite him), his two chamberlains
Will I with wine and wassail so convince
That memory, the warder of the brain,   65
Shall be a fume, and the receipt of reason
A limbeck only. When in swinish sleep
Their drenched natures lie as in a death,
What cannot you and I perform upon
Th' unguarded Duncan? what not put upon   70
His spongy officers, who shall bear the guilt
Of our great quell?

60. **But:** only.—**screw your courage.** The figure is from a crossbow or arbalest. The bow was made of steel, and a mechanical device, sometimes worked with a crank, was attached to the barrel of the gun, by means of which the bow was bent. When fully screwed up, the bowstring would catch in a notch (the *sticking place*) and the weapon was ready to discharge. Lady Macbeth says that all her husband has to do is to get his courage screwed up to the point at which it will remain ready for action without slipping back like an arbalest only partly wound up. **we'll.** Not "we shall," but "we will," expressing determination— "We'll have no failing. I will see to that!" 62, 63. **Whereto...him:** and his hard journey will make him all the readier to sleep, and to sleep soundly.—**chamberlains:** grooms of the bedchamber; officers who had charge of the King's chamber and slept by his bed as a bodyguard. 64. **wassail:** carousal.—**convince:** overpower completely (Latin *convinco*). 65–67. **memory...only.** According to the old physiology, memory resided in the base of the brain at the back of the skull, just above the neck, and reason in the upper part below the dome of the head. The fumes of wine were thought to rise from the stomach to the brain and thus to cause drunkenness. —**limbeck:** the alembic, or cap of the still, into which the fumes rise in the process of distillation. 68. **drenched:** drowned. 70. **put upon:** impute to; charge to, as a crime. 71. **spongy:** drunken (literally, soaking, absorbent). 72. **quell:** killing. Lady Macbeth exalts the murder as a splendid deed, precisely as she had spoken when she bade her husband "put this night's great business into my dispatch" (1.5.68–69).

Here is the same pose, but the genders are reversed, showing that this Macbeth is the motivating force (Freeston, 1997). (Cromwell / LaMancha / Grampian TV / The Kobal Collection)

MACB.   Bring forth men-children only;
For thy undaunted mettle should compose
Nothing but males. Will it not be receiv'd,
When we have mark'd with blood those sleepy two   75
Of his own chamber and us'd their very daggers,
That they have done't?

LADY.   Who dares receive it other,
As we shall make our griefs and clamor roar
Upon his death?

MACB.   I am settled and bend up
Each corporal agent to this terrible feat.   80
Away, and mock the time with fairest show;
False face must hide what the false heart doth know.   *Exeunt.*

---

73. **mettle** (the same word as *metal*): substance, quality. 74. **receiv'd:** accepted as true, believed. 77. **receive it other:** take it otherwise. 78. **As:** in view of the way in which. 79. **settled:** determined, resolute.—**bend up:** stretch to its utmost tension, make quite ready for instant action. The metaphor (from a bow or crossbow) is suggested by Lady Macbeth's words in line 60. 80. **corporal:** bodily. 81. **mock the time:** beguile the world. Here Macbeth returns to his wife the counsel she had given him near the end of scene 5: "to beguile the time, Look like the time."—**show:** appearance, looks and bearing. Macbeth and his wife return to the table and rejoin the royal party.

ACT II

Scene I. [*Inverness. Court of* Macbeth's *Castle.*]

Enter Banquo, *and* Fleance[†] *with a torch before him.*

BAN.   How goes the night, boy?

FLE.   The moon is down; I have not heard the clock.

BAN.   And she goes down at twelve.

FLE.   I take't, 'tis later, sir.

BAN.   Hold, take my sword. There's husbandry in heaven;
      Their candles are all out. Take thee that too.   5
      A heavy summons lies like lead upon me,
      And yet I would not sleep. Merciful powers,
      Restrain in me the cursed thoughts that nature
      Gives way to in repose!

Enter Macbeth, *and a* Servant *with a torch.*

                Give me my sword.
      Who's there?   10

MACB.   A friend.

ACT II. SCENE I.

Banquo, having attended the King to his chamber, has taken leave of him for the night and is on his way to bed. Fleance, his son, acts as his squire. **3. at twelve.** It is past midnight, then, and very dark. The murder, as we shall see later, was committed soon after two o'clock in the morning. Cf. notes on 2.3.26, and 5.1.39. **4. Hold:** a mere interjection, like "here!" (cf. French *tiens*).—**take my sword.** While in attendance on the King, Banquo has worn his sword, as a matter of ceremony (a part of his uniform, so to speak). Being now off duty, he hands it to his squire. Some theorists have tried to find a deep meaning in all this; but it is a simple incident that merely shows that everybody feels safe in Macbeth's castle.—**husbandry:** economy, frugality. Another instance of Banquo's mildly humorous way of speaking. Cf. 1.4.32.—**that too:** his dagger. **6. heavy summons:** a summons to sleep; a feeling of heavy drowsiness. **7. would not sleep.** A vague presentiment makes him reluctant to go to bed; but he has no definite suspicion, whether of Macbeth or of anybody else. **8-9. nature...repose:** to which human nature gives admission in sleep—dreams which we cannot control. On Banquo's dreams (line 20) cf. lines 50–51: "wicked dreams abuse The curtain'd sleep." Banquo's prayer was of the kind common enough in old days. Disagreeable and evil thoughts were supposed to be put into men's minds by demons during the helplessness of the will in slumber. Compare the prayers of Donalbain and his chamberfellow in 2.2.25. The same idea underlies the child's petition "I pray to God my soul to keep" (i.e., "to guard"). *Gives way to* means simply "gives access to," "allows to enter the mind." Banquo has dreamt of the Weird Sisters (whom he regards as evil spirits) and he prays to be spared such dreams tonight. **9.** Banquo is startled by the sudden sight of the torch. As soon as he hears Macbeth's voice, his nervous start passes, and he returns his sword to Fleance.

---

†   Fleance is introduced here as a visual symbol of Banquo's "happier" future as the father of kings. Most performances underscore his innocence by making him a child, although in *Men of Respect* he is a surly teenager. [A.C.]

BAN.	What, sir, not yet at rest? The King's abed.
	He hath been in unusual pleasure and
	Sent forth great largess to your offices.
	This diamond he greets your wife withal	15
	By the name of most kind hostess, and shut up
	In measureless content.
MACB.	Being unprepar'd,
	Our will became the servant to defect,
	Which else should free have wrought.
BAN.	All's well.
	I dreamt last night of the three Weird Sisters.	20
	To you they have show'd some truth.
MACB.	I think not of them.
	Yet when we can entreat an hour to serve,
	We would spend it in some words upon that business,
	If you would grant the time.
BAN.	At your kind'st leisure.
MACB.	If you shall cleave to my consent, when 'tis,	25
	It shall make honor for you.
BAN.	So I lose none
	In seeking to augment it but still keep
	My bosom franchis'd and allegiance clear,
	I shall be counsell'd.
MACB.	Good repose the while.
BAN.	Thanks, sir. The like to you. *Exeunt Banquo [and Fleance].* 30
MACB.	Go bid thy mistress, when my drink is ready,
	She strike upon the bell. Get thee to bed. *Exit [Servant].*

14. **largess:** gifts, gratuities.—**offices:** the kitchen, buttery, and other rooms or buildings in which the servants of a great establishment did their work; hence—the servants of the house. 15. **withal:** with. 16-17. **hostess:** Duncan continues the pleasant humor in which he addresses the Lady in 1.6.10 ("our honor'd hostess") and 31 ("By your leave, hostess").—**shut up...content:** He [Duncan] concluded what he had to say with expressions of unmeasured satisfaction at your hospitality. 18, 19. **Our will... wrought.** Our wish to entertain the King sumptuously (which otherwise would have had free play) was hampered by lack of due preparation. 22. **entreat...serve:** induce the busy times to grant us a little leisure for the purpose. *We* is not the "royal *we*," unconsciously adopted by anticipation: it means simply "you and I."—**serve:** serve our turn. 24. **At your kind'st leisure:** It is very kind of you! Any time when you are at leisure will suit me. 25. **cleave to my consent:** join my party; espouse my interests.—**when 'tis:** when the time comes. 26. **So:** provided that. 27. **still:** ever, always. 28. **franchis'd:** free from blame; void of reproach.—**clear:** untarnished, stainless. 29. **I shall be counsell'd:** I shall be ready to follow your suggestion. Thus even the loyal Banquo admits the possibility that Macbeth may someday become a candidate for the crown without injustice to Duncan or his family. 31. **drink:** the regular draught of warm spiced wine or the like which every Elizabethan or mediæval gentleman and lady took just before going to bed. Such a draught was thought to be eminently wholesome. 32. **the bell:** a signal that all is ready for the murder.

Is this a dagger which I see before me,
The handle toward my hand? Come, let me clutch thee!
I have thee not, and yet I see thee still,   35
Art thou not, fatal vision, sensible
To feeling as to sight? or art thou but
A dagger of the mind, a false creation,
Proceeding from the heat-oppressed brain?
I see thee yet, in form as palpable   40
As this which now I draw.
Thou marshall'st me the way that I was going,
And such an instrument I was to use.
Mine eyes are made the fools o' th' other senses,
Or else worth all the rest. I see thee still;   45
And on thy blade and dudgeon gouts of blood,
Which was not so before. There's no such thing.
It is the bloody business which informs
Thus to mine eyes. Now o'er the one half-world
Nature seems dead, and wicked dreams abuse   50
The curtain'd sleep. Now witchcraft celebrates
Pale Hecate's offerings; and wither'd murder,
Alarum'd by his sentinel, the wolf,
Whose howl's his watch, thus with his stealthy pace,
With Tarquin's ravishing strides, towards his design   55
Moves like a ghost. Thou sure and firm-set earth,
Hear not my steps which way they walk, for fear
Thy very stones prate of my whereabout
And take the present horror from the time,

33–49. This famous soliloquy shows once more the highly imaginative nature of Macbeth, which visualizes to the verge of delirium. Cf. 1.3.130 ff. 36. **fatal:** showing what is fated; sent by fate to lead me to Duncan.—**sensible:** perceptible. 44–45. **Mine eyes...rest:** My eyes have become fools (because they are deluded and see what does not exist) in comparison with my other senses (which are under no such delusion); or else, if the dagger is real, my eyes (which alone perceive it) are worth all my other senses together. 46. **dudgeon:** haft made of dudgeon, which was a kind of fine-grained wood (probably boxwood) much used for this purpose. Macbeth sees and notes each minute detail—so vivid is the vision, so keen his imaginative eye.—**gouts:** big drops. 48. **informs:** gives [false] information (not, takes shape). 50. **wicked dreams.** This sentence is a good commentary on Banquo's prayer in ll. 7–9.—**abuse:** deceive, delude. 51. **The curtain'd sleep:** the sleeper in his curtained bed. 52. **Hecate:** the classical goddess of witchcraft. 53. **Alarum'd:** summoned to action (*all' arme,* "to arms"). 54. **watch.** When the wolf howls, the murderer knows that the time has come for him to act. Hence the howl of the wolf is the murderer's timepiece, striking the hour. Watches (which struck the hours) were large, costly, and elaborate articles of luxury in Shakespeare's time. 55. **strides:** long steps (so as to make as few footfalls as may be). 59. **the present horror:** the dreadful silence which suits the time and the purpose, and which Macbeth wishes should not be disturbed by the sound of his steps.

Which now suits with it. Whiles I threat, he lives;   60
Words to the heat of deeds too cold breath gives.   *A bell rings.*
I go, and it is done. The bell invites me.
Hear it not, Duncan, for it is a knell
That summons thee to heaven, or to hell.   *Exit.*

SCENE II. [*Inverness.* Macbeth's *Castle.*]

Enter Lady [Macbeth].†

LADY.   That which hath made them drunk hath made me bold;
        What hath quench'd them hath given me fire. Hark! Peace!
        It was the owl that shriek'd, the fatal bellman
        Which gives the stern'st good-night. He is about it.
        The doors are open, and the surfeited grooms   5
        Do mock their charge with snores. I have drugg'd their possets,
        That death and nature do contend about them
        Whether they live or die.

MACB.   [*within*] Who's there? What, ho?

LADY.   Alack, I am afraid they have awak'd,   10
        And 'tis not done! Th' attempt, and not the deed,
        Confounds us. Hark! I laid their daggers ready;

60-61. **Whiles...gives:** Talking tends to postpone action that should be carried out in the heat of resolution. Line 60 is broken (and filled out) by the sound of the bell, Lady Macbeth's signal that all is ready (line 32; 2.2.5–14).—**gives.** Such plurals are common, especially when the subject has a collective sense.

SCENE II.
3. **the fatal bellman.** It was custom in London for the bellman or town-crier to visit condemned prisoners on the night before their execution.—**fatal:** sent by the Fates and foretelling death. **The doors:** all the doors through which Macbeth would have to pass, including that of the King's chamber.—**grooms:** the two chamberlains, the grooms of the chamber. 6. **mock their charge:** make a mockery of their duty (of guarding the King).—**possets.** A posset was a curdled drink made of spiced wine or ale, hot milk, grated biscuit, pulp of apples, etc. 7. **That:** so that.—**nature:** their natural vitality; their vital forces. 8. **live or die.** Lady Macbeth does not mean that there is any danger that the chamberlains will not recover, but merely that they are drugged, as we might say, "within an inch of their lives." 11-12. **Th' attempt...us.** *Confounds* means "ruins." Two interpretations are possible: (1) "If he has made the attempt and failed, then we are ruined." (2) "We are ruined, it seems—and that too not by a crime, but by a bungling attempt to commit a crime!" The former is much the better; for what follows shows that Lady Macbeth still hopes that her husband has succeeded in killing Duncan without rousing anybody.

---

†   In *Throne of Blood*, Lady Asaji breaks into a wild dance while waiting for her husband to commit murder—the only moment she acts without intense deliberation. Morrissette shows the murder of Duncan, but characteristically deflates it by having the bound Duncan accidentally fall into the fryer while the Macbeths argue. [A.C.]

He could not miss 'em. Had he not resembled
My father as he slept, I had done't.

Enter Macbeth.

My husband!

MACB. I have done the deed. Didst thou not hear a noise? 15

LADY. I heard the owl scream and the crickets cry.
Did not you speak?

MACB.   When?

LADY.   Now.

MACB.   As I descended?

LADY. Ay.

MACB. Hark!
Who lies i' th' second chamber?

LADY.   Donalbain. 20

MACB. This is a sorry sight.

LADY. A foolish thought, to say a sorry sight.

MACB. There's one did laugh in's sleep, and one cried "Murder!"
That they did wake each other. I stood and heard them.
But they did say their prayers and address'd them 25
Again to sleep.

LADY.   There are two lodg'd together.

MACB. One cried "God bless us!" and "Amen!" the other,
As they had seen me with these hangman's hands,
List'ning their fear. I could not say "Amen!"

---

19. **Hark!** Macbeth does not answer his wife's question, because he is startled by an imaginary noise. After listening for a moment, and finding that it is nothing, he passes over to a different subject. 20. **th' second chamber:** the second from the head of the staircase, Duncan's being the third. 21. **sorry:** wretched, miserable. 23. **There's one,** etc. Macbeth goes on to tell of what he heard as he was passing the second chamber (Donalbain's) on his way back from Duncan's room after committing the murder. He heard two persons speaking, and he had to stand there, waiting outside their door with his bloody hands, until they were quiet again and he could creep by without being heard. 23-25. **in's:** in his.—**That:** so that.—**say their prayers.** Cf. Banquo's prayer against bad dreams (2.1.7–9).—**address'd them:** applied themselves. 26. **two lodg'd together.** "Yes," the Lady answers, "there are two persons lodged in that second chamber, Donalbain and another." The second person may have been an attendant or (perhaps more likely) a young nobleman. It was common for guests to have crowded quarters, even in great houses. 27–28. **God bless us!** and **Amen!** marked the conclusion of the prayers just mentioned.—**As:** as if.—**hangman's:** executioner's. 29. **List'ning their fear:** listening to the prayers they uttered in their alarm at their bad dreams and sudden awaking.—**I could not say "Amen!"** To say "amen" when one heard another utter a blessing was so habitual as to have become instinctive. Macbeth follows his habit, without conscious thought, and finds that for the first time in his life he cannot pronounce the word. His panic at the experience is natural, not naïve. He feels as if his inability were an assurance of damnation.

When they did say "God bless us!"

LADY.   Consider it not so deeply.   30

MACB.   But wherefore could not I pronounce "Amen"?
          I had most need of blessing, and "Amen"
          Stuck in my throat.

LADY.   These deeds must not be thought
          After these ways. So, it will make us mad.

MACB.   Methought I heard a voice cry "Sleep no more!   35
          Macbeth does murder sleep."—the innocent sleep,
          Sleep that knits up the ravell'd sleeve of care,
          The death of each day's life, sore labor's bath,
          Balm of hurt minds, great nature's second course,
          Chief nourisher in life's feast.

LADY.   What do you mean?   40

MACB.   Still it cried "Sleep no more!" to all the house;
          "Glamis hath murder'd sleep, and therefore Cawdor
          Shall sleep no more! Macbeth shall sleep no more!"

LADY.   Who was it that thus cried? Why, worthy Thane,
          You do unbend your noble strength to think   45
          So brainsickly of things. Go get some water
          And wash this filthy witness from your hand.
          Why did you bring these daggers from the place?†
          They must lie there. Go carry them and smear
          The sleepy grooms with blood.

MACB.   I'll go no more.   50
          I am afraid to think what I have done;
          Look on't again I dare not.

---

30. **it:** not "the murder," but "this trivial incident" (his inability to say "amen"). 33-34. **thought:** thought upon, regarded.—**After these ways:** in such a fashion as this (with an agonized dwelling on every little detail, and perplexity as to what it means).—**So:** if we do so.—**mad:** a kind of premonition of Lady Macbeth's final collapse. 37. **knits up:** untangles and straightens out.—**ravell'd:** tangled, snarled.—**sleeve:** skein (as of silk thread). 38. **bath:** because it cures weariness, like a warm bath after toil. 40. **Life's feast** has two courses—food and sleep. Macbeth regards the second as even more sustaining to our nature than the first. The second course was the most substantial part of an Elizabethan dinner. 45-46. **unbend:** relax. It is weak and ignoble of you to harbor such crazy notions. *Brainsick* was a somewhat contemptuous synonym for "insane." 47. **witness:** evidence.

---

†   Lady Macbeth's comment "Why did you bring the daggers from the place?" suggests that she has not seen them before now. Directors sometimes have Macbeth keep his hands hidden behind his back, or in the folds of his gown. Often, Lady Macbeth will reach for his hands; the contrast between her instinct—to comfort Macbeth with human contact—and her anger at his blunder is very powerful. [A.C.]

LADY.   Infirm of purpose!
          Give me the daggers. The sleeping and the dead
          Are but as pictures. 'Tis the eye of childhood
          That fears a painted devil. If he do bleed,   55
          I'll gild the faces of the grooms withal,
          For it must seem their guilt.   *Exit. Knocking within.*

MACB.   Whence is that knocking?
          How is't with me when every noise appals me?
          What hands are here? Ha! they pluck out mine eyes!
          Will all great Neptune's ocean wash this blood   60
          Clean from my hand? No. This my hand will rather
          The multitudinous seas incarnadine,
          Making the green one red.

                    Enter Lady [Macbeth].

LADY.   My hands are of your color, but I shame
          To wear a heart so white. (*Knock.*) I hear a knocking   65
          At the south entry. Retire we to our chamber.
          A little water clears us of this deed.
          How easy is it then! Your constancy
          Hath left you unattended. (*Knock.*) Hark! more knocking.
          Get on your nightgown, lest occasion call us   70
          And show us to be watchers. Be not lost
          So poorly in your thoughts.

MACB.   To know my deed, 'twere best not know myself.   *Knock.*
          Wake Duncan with thy knocking! I would thou couldst!   *Exeunt.*

53-55. **The sleeping…pictures:** The sleeping and the dead are only pictures of living men, and pictures cannot hurt you. "Only a *child* is afraid of a devil that is not real but only *painted!*" 56. **gild** in the sense of "stain" or "smear" (with blood) was common in Shakespeare's time. Cf. "golden blood" (2.3.118) and "red gold." Its use here has a somewhat savage effect (quite intentional), but was not so startling to the Elizabethans as to us; for they were accustomed to punning on the most serious occasions. 57. **within:** behind the scenes. The knocking is outside the gate which separates this tower or wing of the castle from the rest of the building. 62. **The multitudinous seas:** all the seas of the world with their multitude of tumbling waves..—**incarnadine:** turn blood-red. 63. **Making the green one red:** turning the green color of the seas into one universal red. 66. **entry:** entrance. 68-69. **Your constancy…unattended:** Your customary firmness has abandoned you. 70-71. **night-gown:** dressing gown (such as would be thrown on by one called from sleep in haste).—**to be watchers:** not to have gone to bed.—**Be not lost.** Macbeth is once more "rapt," as in 1.3.130. 72. **So poorly:** so weakly; in such a poor-spirited way.

SCENE III. [*Inverness.* Macbeth's *Castle.*]

Enter a Porter. *Knocking within.*[†]

PORTER.   Here's a knocking indeed! If a man were porter of hell gate, he should
have old turning the key. (*Knock.*) Knock, knock, knock! Who's there,
i' th' name of Belzebub? Here's a farmer that hang'd himself on th'
expectation of plenty. Come in time! Have napkins enow about you;
here you'll sweat for't. (*Knock.*) Knock, knock! Who's there, in th' other
devil's name? Faith, here's an equivocator, that could swear in both the
scales against either scale; who committed treason enough for God's
sake, yet could not equivocate to heaven. O, come in, equivocator!
(*Knock.*) Knock, knock, knock! Who's there? Faith, here's an English
tailor come hither for stealing out of a French hose. Come in, tailor.
Here you may roast your goose. (*Knock.*) Knock, knock! Never at
quiet! What are you? But this place is too cold for hell. I'll devil-porter
it no further. I had thought to have let in some of all professions that
go the primrose way to th' everlasting bonfire. (*Knock.*) Anon, anon!
[*Opens the gate.*] I pray you remember the porter.   15

Enter Macduff *and* Lennox.

SCENE III.
The Porter, with just enough wine and wassail left in his brains to make him slow-motioned and
whimsical, enters, rubbing the sleep from his eyes. He grumbles professionally at having so much to do,
and the fancy occurs to him that he is after all not so hard-worked as Satan's gate-keeper. Instantly he
begins to play the part, specifying certain proverbial types of sinners, whom he pretends to let in. Every
one of these types was instantly recognized by the audience as a stock character in the talk of the day. 1.
should: certainly would. 2. **old:** a great deal of. *Old* was in common colloquial use to express emphasis.
3. The farmer had held his wheat for a high price, regardless of the needs of the poor. But the next crop
seemed likely to be heavy, and, desperate at the prospect of a drop in prices, he committed suicide.
Such speculating in foodstuffs has been a favorite subject for denunciation ever since the Middle Ages.
4. **Come in time!** Your arrival is opportune (a mere phrase of welcome).—**napkins:** handkerchiefs.—
enow: enough (usually plural). 5-6. **in th' other devil's name.** The Porter cannot remember the name
of any devil but Belzebub.—**equivocator.** A fling at the Jesuits, who were believed to justify deceptive
ambiguity and "mental reservations." 6-7. **swear...scale:** make an ambiguous statement and swear to
it; swear to a form of words that has two meanings, so that, whichever way the oath is understood by
the hearer, the swearer can say to himself that he meant the other thing. *Scale* has no reference to the
"scales of justice"; it suggests merely the exact balance between the two meanings of the ambiguous
assertion. 7-8. **committed treason enough for God's sake.** The Roman Catholic plots against the
government were, of course, entered into conscientiously by the plotters. Queen Elizabeth had been
excommunicated in 1570 by Pope Pius V, who had released her subjects from their oath of allegiance.
10. **tailor...hose.** Tailors were proverbially said to steal cloth in the process of cutting out clothes for
their customers. The kind of French hose (i.e., breeches) here intended was tight-fitting and required
little cloth. It would take a skilful thief, therefore, to embezzle any. 11. **goose:** the tailor's pressing iron,
so called from its shape and the shape of its handle. 12. **devil-porter it:** act the part of a demon porter
at hell gate. 13. **professions:** occupations. 14. **Anon, anon!** In a moment!—addressed to those who are
knocking. Cf. lines 2–9.

[†]   In *Men of Respect* the Porter character was played by Stephen Wright, a comic noted for his laconic
and deadpan delivery. [A.C.]

MACD.   Was it so late, friend, ere you went to bed,
         That you do lie so late?

PORT.   Faith, sir, we were carousing till the second cock; and drink, sir, is a
         great provoker of three things.

MACD.   What three things does drink especially provoke?   20

PORT.   Marry, sir, nose-painting, sleep, and urine. Lechery, sir, it provokes, and
         unprovokes: it provokes the desire, but it takes away the performance.
         Therefore much drink may be said to be an equivocator with lechery:
         it makes him, and it mars him; it sets him on, and it takes him off;
         it persuades him, and disheartens him; makes him stand to, and not
         stand to; in conclusion, equivocates him in a sleep, and, giving him the
         lie, leaves him.   27

MACD.   I believe drink gave thee the lie last night.

PORT.   That it did, sir, i' the very throat on me; but I requited him for his lie;
         and, I think, being too strong for him, though he took up my legs
         sometime, yet I made a shift to cast him.   31

MACD.   Is thy master stirring?

                              Enter Macbeth.

         Our knocking has awak'd him; here he comes.

LEN.   Good morrow, noble sir.

MACB.   Good morrow, both.

MACD.   Is the King stirring, worthy Thane?

MACB.   Not yet.   35

MACD.   He did command me to call timely on him;
         I have almost slipp'd the hour.

MACB.   I'll bring you to him.

MACD.   I know this is a joyful trouble to you;
         But yet 'tis one.

---

16. **so late.** It is early in the morning (line 37); but it is late for the porter to be on duty. 18. **the second cock.** The times of cockcrow were conventionally fixed as follows: first cock, midnight; second cock, 3 A.M.; third cock, an hour before day. The murder was committed shortly after two o'clock in the morning (5.1.27–28). It is now about four or five o'clock. 28. **gave thee the lie:** floored you and sent you sound asleep—with a pun on *lie*. 29. **i' the very throat on me.** To lie in one's throat was to tell a deep or deliberate lie, as opposed to a mere lip falsehood. The Porter's pun is obvious. *On* in the sense of *of* is extremely common, and so is *of* in the sense of *on*. 30. **took up my legs:** succeeded in getting my feet off the ground. The figure is from wrestling. 31. **made a shift:** contrived, managed.—**cast:** throw, with a pun on *cast* in the sense of "vomit." 36. **timely:** early. 37. **bring:** conduct, escort. 38. **this:** the trouble of conducting me to the King's chamber.

MACB.	The labor we delight in physics pain. 40
	This is the door.
MACD,	I'll make so bold to call,
	For 'tis my limited service. *Exit.*
LEN.	Goes the King hence today?
MACB.	He does; he did appoint so.
LEN.	The night has been unruly. Where we lay,
	Our chimneys were blown down; and, as they say, 45
	Lamentings heard i' th' air, strange screams of death,
	And prophesying, with accents terrible,
	Of dire combustion and confus'd events
	New hatch'd to th' woeful time. The obscure bird
	Clamor'd the livelong night. Some say the earth 50
	Was feverous and did shake.
MACB.	'Twas a rough night.
LEN.	My young remembrance cannot parallel
	A fellow to it.

Enter Macduff.

MACD.	O horror, horror, horror! Tongue nor heart
	Cannot conceive nor name thee!
MACB. AND LEN.	What's the matter? 55
MACD.	Confusion now hath made his masterpiece.
	Most sacrilegious murder hath broke ope
	The Lord's anointed temple and stole thence
	The life o' th' building!
MACB.	What is't you say? the life?
LEN.	Mean you his Majesty? 60

---

40. **The labor,** etc.: when any kind of labor gives us pleasure, the pleasure relieves all the effort that the labor involves. 41. **the door:** not the door of the King's chamber, but a door that leads to the staircase.—**to:** as to. 42. **my limited service:** my specially appointed duty. 43. **appoint:** arrange, plan. 46. **Lamentings heard i' th' air.** Such prodigies were regularly supposed to announce or accompany the death of princes or great men. 48. **combustion:** tumult and disorder in the state. 49. **hatch'd to.** As we say "A son was born to him."—**the óbscure bird:** the bird of darkness; the owl (cf. 2.2.3–4). 51. **feverous.** Malarial fever (fever and ague) was prevalent in Shakespeare's England, for there were immense undrained marshes, and the chills and shaking that accompany it are often used in metaphor. Cf. "life's fitful fever" (3.2.23); "Then comes my fit again" (3.4.21); "the fits o' th' season" (4.2.17). 56. **Confusion:** destruction. 58. **The Lord's anointed temple:** the sacred body of the King, which is not only God's temple, but God's *anointed* temple. Our bodies are God's temples according to the passage in *2 Corinthians,* iv.16: "Ye are the temple of the living God." Anointing was a part of the ceremony of coronation.

MACD.   Approach the chamber, and destroy your sight
         With a new Gorgon. Do not bid me speak.
         See, and then speak yourselves.   *Exeunt Macbeth and Lennox.*
                           Awake, awake!
         Ring the alarm bell. Murder and treason!
         Banquo and Donalbain! Malcolm! awake!   65
         Shake off this downy sleep, death's counterfeit,
         And look on death itself! Up, up, and see
         The great doom's image! Malcolm! Banquo!
         As from your graves rise up and walk like sprites
         To countenance this horror! Ring the bell!   *Bell rings.* 70

                   Enter Lady [Macbeth].

LADY.   What's the business,
         That such a hideous trumpet calls to parley
         The sleepers of the house? Speak, speak!

MACD.   O gentle lady,
         'Tis not for you to hear what I can speak!
         The repetition in a woman's ear   75
         Would murder as it fell.

                     Enter Banquo.

                    O Banquo, Banquo,
         Our royal master's murder'd!

LADY.   Woe, alas!
         What, in our house?

BAN.   Too cruel anywhere.
         Dear Duff, I prithee contradict thyself
         And say it is not so.   80

               Enter Macbeth, Lennox, *and* Ross.

MACB.   Had I but died an hour before this chance,
         I had liv'd a blessed time; for from this instant
         There's nothing serious in mortality;
         All is but toys; renown and grace is dead;

---

62. **Gorgon.** The horrible sight will, like the Gorgon Medusa, turn his eyes to stone. We still speak of "a stony stare." 64. **alarum bell:** literally, the bell that calls to arms (*all' arme*). 66. **counterfeit:** imitation, likeness. 68. **great doom's image:** a sight as dreadful as the Day of Doom. *Image* means "exact likeness," as when we say "The girl is the image of her mother." 69. **As from your graves.** Macduff dwells upon the thought of the Day of Doom, when the dead shall arise in their shrouds.—**like sprites:** in the guise of spirits (all in white). Cf. 1.3.9; 1.7.21; 3.4.100; 4.1.87. 70. **To countenance this horror:** to keep the horrid sight in countenance; that is, to accord with it, to give it a proper setting. 75. **repetition:** recital, report. 83. **nothing serious in mortality:** nothing worth while in human life. 84. **toys:** trifles.—**grace:** goodness, virtue.

The wine of life is drawn, and the mere lees   85
Is left this vault to brag of.

Enter Malcolm *and* Donalbain.

Don.   What is amiss?

Macb.   You are, and do not know't.
            The spring, the head, the fountain of your blood
            Is stopp'd, the very source of it is stopp'd.

Macd.   Your royal father's murder'd.

Mal.   O, by whom?   90

Len.   Those of his chamber, as it seem'd, had done't.
            Their hands and faces were all badg'd with blood;
            So were their daggers, which unwip'd we found
            Upon their pillows.
            They star'd and were distracted. No man's life   95
            Was to be trusted with them.

Macb.   O, yet I do repent me of my fury
            That I did kill them.

Macd.   Wherefore did you so?

Macb.   Who can be wise, amaz'd, temp'rate and furious,
            Loyal and neutral, in a moment? No man.   100
            The expedition of my violent love
            Outrun the pauser, reason. Here lay Duncan,
            His silver skin lac'd with his golden blood,
            And his gash'd stabs look'd like a breach in nature
            For ruin's wasteful entrance; there, the murderers, 105

85-86. **The wine of life...brag of:** Everything that gave zest to existence is gone, now that Duncan is dead, and this world (like an empty wine vault) has nothing left of its vaunted pleasures—nothing but the nauseous dregs of life. 88. **head:** well-head or source. Macbeth uses four synonyms. We have already noted how apt he is to dwell upon an idea and express it in different figures of speech (see 1.7.4). 92. **badg'd:** marked. The figure comes from the badges or cognizances which retainers of great houses were accustomed to wear. These consisted usually of the arms or crest of the head of the house. 95. **They star'd and were distracted:** that is, when roused from their heavy, drugged sleep. Macbeth killed the chamberlains before they had a chance to say a word (see 3.6.12–13). 97. **fury:** madness, frenzy (not, wrath). Cf. lines 99–100. Macduff's question implies neither anger nor suspicion. He simply regrets that it is not possible to interrogate the grooms. Yet even here we find him instinctively uneasy with regard to Macbeth, and this feeling grows steadily (cf. 2.4.37–38) until he becomes Macbeth's chief opponent. 99. **amaz'd:** utterly confused in mind, mentally paralyzed (not, as in modern English, surprised).—**temp'rate:** self-controlled, calm. Cf. 4.3.92.—**furious:** frenzied. 101. **expedition:** haste. 103. **silver skin.** The figure gives a vivid idea of bloodless pallour. Blood is called golden because it is red, and "red gold" is a common expression. —**lac'd:** marked as if in the figures of lace. 104. **a breach.** The figure is of a city wall in which assailants have made a breach by which they can enter and lay waste the town. —**nature:** life, vitality. 105. **wasteful:** destructive.

Steep'd in the colors of their trade, their daggers
Unmannerly breech'd with gore. Who could refrain
That had a heart to love and in that heart
Courage to make's love known?

LADY.   Help me hence, ho![†]

MACD.   Look to the lady.

MAL.   [*aside to Donalbain*] Why do we hold our tongues,   110
That most may claim this argument for ours?

DON.   [*aside to Malcolm*] What should be spoken here, where our fate,
Hid in an auger hole, may rush and seize us?
Let's away.
Our tears are not yet brew'd.

MAL.   [*aside to Donalbain*]   Nor our strong sorrow   115
Upon the foot of motion.

BAN.   Look to the lady.
                                    [*Lady Macbeth is carried out.*]
And when we have our naked frailties hid,
That suffer in exposure, let us meet
And question this most bloody piece of work,
To know it further. Fears and scruples shake us.   120
In the great hand of God I stand, and thence
Against the undivulg'd pretence I fight
Of treasonous malice.

MACD.   And so do I.

ALL.   So all.

---

107. **Unmannerly breech'd:** covered in an unseemly fashion.—**refrain:** hold one's self back, check one's impulse. 109. **'s love:** his love. 111. **That...ours:** who have the best right to talk on this subject. *Argument* is common in the sense of "topic," "plot of a play," "subject matter." 112. **here:** emphatic. This castle—fatal to our family—is no place for our laments. We are in danger ourselves, and must first provide for our own safety. 113. **Hid in an auger hole:** lurking in some unsuspected hiding place. 115. **tears...brew'd:** the time has not come for us to weep for our father. 115-116. **Nor...motion:** nor has our grief, strong as it is, yet begun to act—it is felt, not shown. 117. **our...hid:** clothed our poor shivering bodies. 120. **scruples:** vague suspicions. 121. **thence:** making God's strength my fortress. 122. **undivulg'd pretence:** the as yet undiscovered purpose of the traitor (whoever he is) who has contrived this foul deed. Banquo has, as yet, no distinct suspicion of Macbeth.

---

†   The choice of whether to have Lady Macbeth truly faint here, or merely pretend, is a key moment for the development of her character. In Polanski's version, the delicate Lady Macbeth is overcome by hearing the gory details, while Welles' heroine is clearly distracting the other nobles from Macbeth's increasing frenzy. [A.C.]

MACB.   Let's briefly put on manly readiness
         And meet i' th' hall together.

ALL.   Well contented.   125

                  Exeunt [all but Malcolm and Donalbain].

MAL.   What will you do? Let's not consort with them.
         To show an unfelt sorrow is an office
         Which the false man does easy. I'll to England.

DON.   To Ireland I. Our separated fortune
         Shall keep us both the safer. Where we are,   130
         There's daggers in men's smiles; the near in blood,
         The nearer bloody.

MAL.   This murderous shaft that's shot
         Hath not yet lighted, and our safest way
         Is to avoid the aim. Therefore to horse!
         And let us not be dainty of leave-taking   135
         But shift away. There's warrant in that theft
         Which steals itself when there's no mercy left.   *Exeunt.*

---

124. **briefly:** quickly, hurriedly.—**put on manly readiness:** clothe ourselves properly (not, put on our armor). *Ready* and *unready* were the ordinary adjectives for "dressed" and "undressed." *Manly readiness* suggests also "self-possession"—that frame of mind that shall make us ready for action. 125. **Well contented:** well and good. 127. **office:** function. 128. **the false man:** i.e., any false man. The young Princes suspect everybody. Macbeth, as their near kinsman and a probable candidate for the throne, seems to them likely to have contrived the murder (lines 131–132), but they are by no means certain that Banquo and Macduff are not his accomplices. 129. **Our...fortune:** this separation for our fortune; the fact that we try our luck separately. 131-132. **the near...bloody.** *Near* is a comparative: The nearer one of these nobles is to us in kindred, the more likely he is to wish to murder us. The remark, though specially applicable to the present circumstances, is proverbial in tone, and suggests the prophesy in *Matthew*, x.36: "A man's foes shall be they of his own household." 132-133. **This...lighted:** This arrow of murder is still in the air; this murderous plot has not yet attained its full object (our death as well as our father's). 135. **dainty of:** punctilious about. 136. **shift away:** steal away unperceived.—**warrant:** justification. A man has a right to steal when what he takes away is merely *himself* from a place of deadly peril.

SCENE IV. [*Inverness. Without* Macbeth's *Castle.*]

Enter Ross *with an* Old Man.

OLD MAN. Threescore and ten I can remember well;
Within the volume of which time I have seen
Hours dreadful and things strange; but this sore night
Hath trifled former knowings.

ROSS.   Ah, good father,
Thou seest the heavens, as troubled with man's act,   5
Threaten his bloody stage. By th' clock 'tis day,
And yet dark night strangles the travelling lamp.
Is't night's predominance, or the day's shame,
That darkness does the face of earth entomb
When living light should kiss it?

OLD MAN.   'Tis unnatural,   10
Even like the deed that's done. On Tuesday last
A falcon, tow'ring in her pride of place,
Was by a mousing owl hawk'd at and kill'd.

ROSS. And Duncan's horses (a thing most strange and certain),
Beauteous and swift, the minions of their race,   15
Turn'd wild in nature, broke their stalls, flung out,
Contending 'gainst obedience, as they would make
War with mankind.

OLD MAN.   'Tis said they eat each other.

ROSS. They did so, to th' amazement of mine eyes
That look'd upon't.

SCENE IV.
This scene takes place on the same day as scene 3, but much has occurred in the interval. The young princes have made their escape; the electors have met and chosen Macbeth king, and he and his wife have set out for Scone for the coronation. The place of the scene is still Inverness, either just outside the walls of Macbeth's castle or in one of the courtyards. 1. The **old man** is a person of some rank, as well as of long and varied experience. His age gives him the wisdom of a seer, as we may infer from lines 40–41. His benign and dignified figure serves as a kind of chorus to the tragedy, and his prophetic speech at the end brings the stormy Second Act to a calm and impressive close. 1–4. The omens and prodigies are continued from 2.3.44–51. They are taken from Holinshed's account of the murder of King Duff, and such things are often recorded in similar cases. 1–31.—**sore:** dreadful.—**trifled former knowings:** made all my previous experiences seem trivial.—**father.** Used in addressing any venerable man. 6. **his bloody stage:** this earth, on which man performs his bloody deeds. 7. **the travelling lamp:** the travelling torch (of Phœbus, the sun). 8–10. **Is't…kiss it?** Is the darkness due to Night's having become more powerful in the world than Day, or to Day's hiding his face in shame? 12. **tow'-ring…place:** soaring proudly, and at the very summit (or highest pitch) of her flight. 13. **mousing owl:** an owl, whose natural prey is mice, not falcons. 15. **minions of their race:** the darlings of the horse tribe; the finest of all horses. Cf. 1.2.19. 16–17. **flung out:** kicked and plunged wildly.—**as:** as if. 19. **amazement:** stupefaction. Cf. 2.3.114.

Enter Macduff.

Here comes the good Macduff.   20
How goes the world, sir, now?

MACD.   Why, see you not?

ROSS.   Is't known who did this more than bloody deed?

MACD.   Those that Macbeth hath slain.

ROSS.   Alas, the day!
What good could they pretend?

MACD.   They were suborn'd.
Malcolm and Donalbain, the King's two sons,   25
Are stol'n away and fled, which puts upon them
Suspicion of the deed.

ROSS.   'Gainst nature still!
Thriftless ambition, that wilt raven up
Thine own live's means. Then 'tis most like
The sovereignty will fall upon Macbeth.   30

MACD.   He is already nam'd, and gone to Scone
To be invested.

ROSS.   Where is Duncan's body?

MACD.   Carried to Colmekill,
The sacred storehouse of his predecessors
And guardian of their bones.

ROSS.   Will you to Scone?   35

MACD.   No, cousin, I'll to Fife.

ROSS.   Well, I will thither.

MACD.   Well, may you see things well done there. Adieu,
Lest our old robes sit easier than our new.

---

20. Macduff comes out of the castle (or out of the hall into the courtyard) from the meeting of the electors.
24. **pretend:** intend to gain for themselves by such an act.—**suborn'd:** secretly bribed or induced—used of "procuring" any crime, not, as in the modern idiom, limited to perjury and treason.—**'Gainst nature still:** continuing the Old Man's thought in lines 10–11. 28. **Thriftless:** improvident.—**raven up:** devour ravenously. In their mad ambition to reign, they have destroyed all their own prospects of succeeding to the throne. 30. **upon Macbeth:** who stands next in succession. 31. **nam'd:** elected (by the council of nobles).—**Scone:** where the Scottish kings were regularly crowned. 32. **invested:** clothed with sovereignty (at the coronation). 36. **Fife:** Macduff's own home. 37. **well done:** May the coronation of Macbeth really be a good thing for Scotland. Macduff fears (as the next line shows) that Macbeth's reign may be less agreeable to the nobility than the mild sway of Duncan. His words have no suggestion that he suspects Macbeth's guilt.

Ross.   Farewell, father.

Old Man.   God's benison go with you, and with those   40
             That would make good of bad, and friends of foes.   *Exeunt omnes.*

Act III

Scene I. [*Forres. The Palace.*]

Enter Banquo.

Ban.   Thou hast it now—King, Cawdor, Glamis, all,
             As the Weird Women promis'd; and I fear
             Thou play'dst most foully for't. Yet it was said
             It should not stand in thy posterity,
             But that myself should be the root and father   5
             Of many kings. If there come truth from them,
             (As upon thee, Macbeth, their speeches shine),
             Why, by the verities on thee made good,
             May they not be my oracles as well
             And set me up in hope? But, hush, no more.   10

             Sennet sounded. Enter Macbeth, *as* King; Lady [Macbeth, *as*
             Queen]; Lennox, Ross, Lords, *and* Attendants.

40-41. God's benison…foes: God's blessing go with you both—and with all other well-meaning and unsuspicious persons who, like you, insist on regarding bad men as good and your foes as your friends.

Act III. Scene I.
Some months have elapsed since the coronation. The young princes have reached places of safety—Malcolm in England and Donalbain in Ireland—and reports have come back to Scotland that they accuse Macbeth of the murder (lines 30–33). Banquo, who has had time to think and has heard these reports, fears they are true; but the time for action has not yet come. Macduff has grown more and more hostile to Macbeth and keeps away from court. The King himself, now well established in power, has begun to suffer both from remorse and from fear—fear of Banquo especially. 3. **Thou play'dst most foully.** Cf. Lady Macbeth's words (1.5.17–18): Wouldst not play false, And yet wouldst wrongly win. In no other play of Shakespeare's, perhaps, are there so many echoes as in *Macbeth.*—**most foully for't.** Shakespeare's departure from Holinshed is significant. As King James's supposed ancestor, Banquo must be a loyal man. 6. **truth.** Compare Banquo's half-jesting exclamation: "What, can the devil speak true?" (1.3.107). 7. **As…shine:** as [well may be the case, for] upon thee their speeches are not only fulfilled, but *brilliantly* fulfilled.—**shine** (emphatic): shine with the lustre of splendid reality. 10. **Sennet:** a series of notes on a trumpet announcing the entrance of a person of high degree or of a stately procession.

---

†   Welles uses camera angles to emphasize Macbeth's ascension to power, shooting from behind and above to make the courtiers look tiny and insignificant. Morrissette uses a collage of images to show the Macbeths, now owners of Duncan's Donuts, modernizing the restaurant, buying a new house and dressing in increasingly elaborate fashions of the 1970s. [A.C.]

MACB.   Here's our chief guest.

LADY.   If he had been forgotten,
         It had been as a gap in our great feast,
         And all-thing unbecoming.

MACB.   Tonight we hold a solemn supper, sir,
         And I'll request your presence.

BAN.   Let your Highness   15
         Command upon me, to the which my duties
         Are with a most indissoluble tie
         For ever knit.

MACB.   Ride you this afternoon?

BAN.   Ay, my good lord.

MACB.   We should have else desir'd your good advice   20
         (Which still hath been both grave and prosperous)
         In this day's council; but we'll take tomorrow.
         Is't far you ride?

BAN.   As far, my lord, as will fill up the time
         'Twixt this and supper. Go not my horse the better, 25
         I must become a borrower of the night
         For a dark hour or twain.

MACB.   Fail not our feast.

BAN.   My lord, I will not.

MACB.   We hear our bloody cousins are bestow'd
         In England and in Ireland, not confessing   30
         Their cruel parricide, filling their hearers
         With strange invention. But of that tomorrow,
         When therewithal we shall have cause of state

---

13. **all-thing:** altogether. 14. **solemn supper:** a supper of ceremony, a state supper. 15. **I'll.** Macbeth's use of *I* instead of the royal *we* gives the invitation a personal quality that makes it especially gracious. 16. **Command:** in emphatic contrast with Macbeth's word *request*. Royal invitations are still called commands.—**the which:** i.e., your royal commands. The antecedent noun (as often) is implied in the verb. 18. **Ride you this afternoon?** In the dialogue that follows, three questions stand out with sinister emphasis among the gracious words of the King: "Ride you this afternoon?" "Is't far you ride?" "Goes Fleance with you?" Macbeth has already planned the murder of Banquo and Fleance, and Banquo's replies give him what information he needs to carry out the plot that very night. All his compliments are mere wrappings for these three questions. 21. **still:** always.—**grave and prosperous:** weighty and good in its results. Note the implication that there have been previous councils: Macbeth has now reigned for some time. 25-27. **Go...twain:** Unless my horse goes too fast to make that necessary, I shall have to continue my ride an hour or two after dark. *The better* means "better than *that*," i.e., "too well for *that*" (too well to keep me out so late). 29. **cousins:** Malcolm and Donalbain.—**are bestow'd:** have taken refuge. 32. **strange invention.** They have been accusing Macbeth of the murder, and the report has reached Scotland. 33. **there-with-al:** therewith, besides that.—**cause of state:** public business.

Craving us jointly. Hie you to horse. Adieu,
Till you return at night. Goes Fleance with you?   35

BAN.   Ay, my good lord. Our time does call upon's.

MACB.   I wish your horses swift and sure of foot,
And so I do commend you to their backs.
Farewell.   *Exit Banquo.*
Let every man be master of his time   40
Till seven at night. To make society
The sweeter welcome, we will keep ourself
Till supper time alone. While then, God be with you.
        Exeunt Lords [and others. Manent Macbeth and a Servant].
Sirrah, a word with you. Attend those men
Our pleasure?   45

SERV.   They are, my lord, without the palace gate.

MACB.   Bring them before us.   *Exit Servant.*
                    To be thus is nothing,
But to be safely thus. Our fears in Banquo
Stick deep, and in his royalty of nature
Reigns that which would be fear'd. 'Tis much he dares,   50
And to that dauntless temper of his mind
He hath a wisdom that doth guide his valor
To act in safety. There is none but he
Whose being I do fear; and under him
My Genius is rebuk'd, as it is said   55
Mark Antony's was by Cæsar. He chid the Sisters
When first they put the name of King upon me,
And bade them speak to him. Then, prophet-like,
They hail'd him father to a line of kings.
Upon my head they plac'd a fruitless crown   60

---

34. **Craving us jointly:** requiring both your attention and mine. Thus Macbeth associates himself with Banquo in a very particular manner, as if they had common interests which the others did not share. Banquo may well think that the business meant is the prophecy made by the Weird Sisters to him. 36. **Our time...upon's:** time summons us to depart. 39. **commend you:** entrust you—with my best wishes. 41-43. **To make...alone:** In order that company (your society) may be all the more agreeable to me, I will deprive myself of it for a time.—**The sweeter welcome:** the more sweetly welcome to me.—**ourself:** the regular emphatic and reflexive form of the royal *we*.—**While then, God be with you:** Until then, good-bye. *Good-bye* is simply a clipped form of *God be wi' ye*. 45. **Sirrah.** Often used in addressing a servant, an inferior, or a child (4.2.30). 47. **To be thus:** to be King. 48. **But to be safely thus:** without being (unless I am to be) safe on my throne. Macbeth finds that the assassination has not "trammelled up the consequence" (1.7.3). The general fear that he expressed in his soliloquy—that in killing Duncan he might be "teaching bloody instructions"—has now become specific: he thinks that Banquo may plot his murder. 50. **that:** that quality (i.e., ambition).—**would be:** requires to be. 51. **to:** in addition to, besides.—**temper:** quality, disposition. 52. **Genius:** guardian spirit.—**rebuk'd:** put to shame, abashed, cowed.

And put a barren sceptre in my gripe,
Thence to be wrench'd with an unlineal hand,
No son of mine succeeding. If't be so,
For Banquo's issue have I fil'd my mind;
For them the gracious Duncan have I murder'd;   65
Put rancours in the vessel of my peace
Only for them, and mine eternal jewel
Given to the common enemy of man
To make them kings, the seed of Banquo kings!
Rather than so, come, Fate, into the list,   70
And champion me to th' utterance! Who's there?

         Enter Servant *and two* Murderers.

Now go to the door and stay there till we call.   *Exit Servant.*
Was it not yesterday we spoke together?

MURDERERS.   It was, so please your Highness.

MACB.   Well then, now
Have you consider'd of my speeches? Know   75
That it was he, in the times past, which held you
So under fortune, which you thought had been
Our innocent self. This I made good to you
In our last conference, pass'd in probation with you
How you were borne in hand, how cross'd; the instruments;   80
Who wrought with them; and all things else that might

---

62. **with:** by. 64. **fil'd:** defiled. 66. **Put rancours...peace.** Before the murder, Macbeth was at peace with God and man and with his own conscience: now he feels at enmity with all three. *Rancour* is the strongest possible word for "malignant enmity." The figure is of a vessel full of some wholesome liquid (like milk) into which poison has been poured. Cf. the "poison'd chalice" (1.7.11) and 'the milk of human kindness' (1.5.13). 67. **mine eternal jewel:** my immortal treasure (my soul). Another echo of the soliloquy before the murder (1.7.7). 70. **list:** the lists (arena for combat or competition [A.C.]). 71. **champion me:** meet me face to face in combat as a champion meets his opponent.—**to th' utterance:** *à outrance,* in a duel to the death. Macbeth, though a strong fatalist, determines to attempt the overthrow of Fate in one particular point.—**Who's there?** A summons to the servant who attends in the lobby. 74. The murderers are not mere hired assassins. They are Scottish gentlemen of desperate fortunes, and have hitherto been Macbeth's enemies, for to him they have ascribed their troubles. In a previous interview, however, he has convinced them that it was Banquo who had wronged them; and he now spurs them to revenge. Thus they are sharply distinguished from the brutal hirelings who butcher Lady Macduff and her son (4.2.76–81). 74. **your Highness:** your Majesty. 76. **it was he:** i.e., Banquo. As in the great soliloquy (1.7), *his* is used in line 4, and *he* in line 12, and the name *Duncan* is not mentioned until line 16—so here Banquo's name occurs first in line 83. 76-77.—**held you...So under fortune:** kept you down in your fortunes; thwarted your careers. 78. **made good:** proved. 79. **pass'd in probation with you:** I reviewed the facts with you and gave you the proofs. The object of *pass'd* is what follows, "How you were borne in hand," etc. 80. **borne in hand:** deluded (by Banquo). To bear a man in hand is not merely to deceive him, but to do so by means of a regular course of treachery; to play the hypocrite with him; to nourish false hopes, etc.—**cross'd:** thwarted in all your efforts.—**the instruments:** the tools. Macbeth says that he named the very agents by means of whom Banquo had worked against them.

To half a soul and to a notion craz'd
Say 'Thus did Banquo.'

1. MUR.   You made it known to us.

MACB.   I did so; and went further, which is now
Our point of second meeting. Do you find   85
Your patience so predominant in your nature
That you can let this go? Are you so gospell'd
To pray for this good man and for his issue,
Whose heavy hand hath bow'd you to the grave
And beggar'd yours for ever?

1. MUR.   We are men, my liege.   90

MACB.   Ay, in the catalogue ye go for men,
As hounds and greyhounds, mongrels, spaniels, curs,
Shoughs, water-rugs, and demi-wolves are clipt
All by the name of dogs. The valued file
Distinguishes the swift, the slow, the subtle,   95
The housekeeper, the hunter, every one
According to the gift which bounteous nature
Hath in him clos'd; whereby he does receive
Particular addition, from the bill
That writes them all alike; and so of men.   100
Now, if you have a station in the file,
Not i' th' worst rank of manhood, say't;
And I will put that business in your bosoms
Whose execution takes your enemy off,

---

82. **half a soul:** even to one who had only half a man's wits.—**notion:** mind, intellect. 83. **Banquo.** With this word, we learn for the first time whom Macbeth has been accusing. 85. **Our point of second meeting:** the point or purpose of this second meeting. 86. **patience:** passive endurance.—**so predominant:** so much more powerful than all other qualities. *Predominant* is an astrological term applied to that planet which is powerful above all others at a given time. 87. **so gospell'd:** so tamely submissive to the gospel precept to "love your enemies, bless them that curse you, do good to them that hate you, and pray for them which despitefully use you and persecute you" (*Matthew,* v.44). 88. **To:** as to.—**for his issue.** An intensely significant addition. Cf. lines 135–138. 90. **yours:** your families and descendants.—**liege:** liege lord, sovereign. 91. **in the catalogue:** in a mere list; as we might say "in the census."—**go for:** pass for, count for. 93. **Shoughs:** a kind of shaggy Iceland dog, in favor as a lady's pet in Shakespeare's time. Pronounced *shocks.*—**water-rugs:** some kind of shaggy water-dog.—**demi-wolves:** a cross between wolf and dog.—**clipt:** called. 94. **The valued file:** the list which (as opposed to an indiscriminate *catalogue*) notes the *valuable quality* which distinguishes each breed. 96. **housekeeper:** the keeper, or guard, of the house; the watchdog. 98. **Hath in him clos'd:** has put into him; endowed him with.—**whereby:** by virtue of which. 99-100. **Particular...alike:** a special name or title, in distinction from the list (*bill*) that writes them all down indiscriminately as *dogs. Bill* was applied to almost any kind of document.—**from:** away from—and so, "in opposition to," "in distinction from." 101. **file:** the same word used in line 94 for "list"; but it immediately suggests to Macbeth the military sense, and hence he goes on to speak of *rank* in the next verse. 104. **takes your enemy off.** Two motives are suggested for killing Banquo—revenge and the hope of winning the King's favor. *Takes off* is the same phrase used by Macbeth in 1.7.20—another echo.

	Grapples you to the heart and love of us,
	Who wear our health but sickly in his life,
	Which in his death were perfect.

2. MUR.   I am one, my liege,
Whom the vile blows and buffets of the world
Have so incens'd that I am reckless what
I do to spite the world.

1. MUR.   And I another,
So weary with disasters, tugg'd with fortune,
That I would set my life on any chance,
To mend it or be rid on't.

MACB.   Both of you
Know Banquo was your enemy.

MURDERERS.   True, my lord.

MACB.   So is he mine; and in such bloody distance
That every minute of his being thrusts
Against my near'st of life; and though I could
With barefac'd power sweep him from my sight
And bid my will avouch it, yet I must not,
For certain friends that are both his and mine,
Whose loves I may not drop, but wail his fall
Who I myself struck down. And thence it is
That I to your assistance do make love,
Masking the business from the common eye
For sundry weighty reasons.

2. MUR.   We shall, my lord,
Perform what you command us.

1. MUR.   Though our lives—

MACB.   Your spirits shine through you. Within this hour at most
I will advise you where to plant yourselves,
Acquaint you with the perfect spy o' th' time,

Line numbers: 105, 110, 115, 120, 125

---

106. **wear...life:** have but feeble health so long as he is alive (since his life endangers mine). 111. **tugg'd:** pulled about, roughly handled.—**with:** by, as in line 63. 112. **set:** stake, venture.—**chance:** cast of the dice, hazard. 115. **bloody distance:** mortal enmity. 116. **being:** existence (as in line 54). 117. **my near'st of life:** my most vital spot. Banquo's mere existence is a dagger, set at Macbeth's breast over his heart and pressed in steadily and inexorably minute by minute. 118. **With bare-fac'd power:** with frank and undisguised exercise of my royal authority. 119. **avouch it:** authorize the deed; justify it. 121. **For:** because of. —**may not:** must not. 121-122. **but wail...down:** but [I must] seem to lament the death of him whom I myself slew. 127. **Your spirits,** etc.: Your courage and resolution appear in your sparkling eyes and eager faces. 128. **advise you:** send you information. 129. **with...time:** with absolutely full and exact indication of the time when the deed should be done.—**spy:** literally, espial, observation.

The moment on't; for't must be done to-night,   130
And something from the palace; always thought
That I require a clearness; and with him,
To leave no rubs nor botches in the work,
Fleance his son, that keeps him company,
Whose absence is no less material to me   135
Than is his father's, must embrace the fate
Of that dark hour. Resolve yourselves apart;
I'll come to you anon.

MURDERERS.   We are resolv'd, my lord.

MACB.   I'll call upon you straight. Abide within.   [*Exeunt Murderers.*]
It is concluded. Banquo, thy soul's flight,   140
If it find heaven, must find it out to-night.   *Exit.*

SCENE II. [*Forres. The Palace.*]

Enter Macbeth's Lady *and a* Servant.

LADY.   Is Banquo gone from court?

SERV.   Ay, madam, but returns again tonight.

LADY.   Say to the King I would attend his leisure
For a few words.†

SERV.   Madam, I will.   *Exit.*

LADY.   Naught's had, all's spent,
Where our desire is got without content.   5
'Tis safer to be that which we destroy
Than by destruction dwell in doubtful joy.

---

131. **something from:** at some distance from. Cf. note on line 100.—**always thought:** it being always understood. 132. **I:** emphatic.—**clearness:** complete freedom from risk of being suspected. 133. **rubs nor botches:** flaws or defects (due to bungling). Macbeth wishes the murderers "to make a clean job of it." A rub in bowling is any impediment that deflects or hinders the course of the bowl; hence, also, the course thus impeded or thwarted. 137. **Resolve yourselves apart:** Make up your minds, by conferring in private, whether you will undertake the business or not. 139. **straight:** straightway, immediately. 140–141. Cf. 2.1.63–64: Hear it not, Duncan, for it is a knell / That summons thee to heaven, or to hell.

SCENE II.
This scene is practically continuous with scene 1. It begins—as that scene ends—with "Banquo." He is the burden of Lady Macbeth's thoughts as of her husband's. 5. **content:** happiness.

---

†   In Kurosawa, Waashizu (Macbeth) at first insists on declaring Miki (Banquo) his heir. He changes his mind, however, when Asaji (Lady Macbeth) declares she is pregnant (her later miscarriage causes her insanity, rather than her guilty conscience). 3.2 becomes, therefore, the height of her power, rather than the first moment that Macbeth acts independently of her. [A.C.]

Enter Macbeth.

How now, my lord? Why do you keep alone,
Of sorriest fancies your companions making,
Using those thoughts which should indeed have died   10
With them they think on? Things without all remedy
Should be without regard. What's done is done.

MACB.   We have scotch'd the snake, not kill'd it.
She'll close, and be herself, whilst our poor malice
Remains in danger of her former tooth.   15
But let the frame of things disjoint, both the worlds suffer,
Ere we will eat our meal in fear and sleep
In the affliction of these terrible dreams
That shake us nightly. Better be with the dead,
Whom we, to gain our peace, have sent to peace,   20
Than on the torture of the mind to lie
In restless ecstasy. Duncan is in his grave;
After life's fitful fever he sleeps well.
Treason has done his worst. Nor steel nor poison,
Malice domestic, foreign levy, nothing,   25
Can touch him further.

LADY.   Come on.
Gentle my lord, sleek o'er your rugged looks;
Be bright and jovial among your guests tonight.

---

9. **sorriest:** most paltry, despicable. 10. **Using:** associating with. 11–12. **them.** Duncan alone is meant, but the plural is used in the common generalizing sense—**without all:** beyond all. 12. The tragic element consists in the fact that it is *not* "done." Cf. Macbeth's scruple before the murder (1.7.1): "If it were done when 'tis done"; and the Lady's own words (5.1.57): "What's done cannot be undone." 13. **scotch'd:** slashed, gashed. 14. **close:** come together again; join and be as strong as ever. It was a common notion that a snake, when cut in two, will reunite unless the head is crushed. Macbeth now counts the murdered Duncan among his enemies. The snake is a figure for all those who stand or have stood in the way of his getting, holding, and enjoying the crown, and of these Banquo (so he feels) is one. 14–15. **our poor malice...tooth:** our feeble enmity has proved of no avail and leaves us exposed to the same danger (from the serpent) as when it was uninjured. 16–19. **let...disjoint:** let the whole fabric (or structure) of the universe go to pieces; let chaos come again.—**both the worlds:** this world and the next.—**suffer:** die, perish. *Suffer* in the sense of "suffer death" is common. 21. **on...lie:** to find that our bed is a rack on which we are stretched in torment. 22. **In restless ecstasy:** in a frenzy of sleeplessness and unrest. 23. **life's fitful fever.** Life seems to Macbeth a tormenting malarial fever (see note on 2.3.66)—now hot, now cold, never at rest: only in death is there peace (cf. 4.3.179). 24. **his:** the usual genitive of *it*. 25. **Malice domestic, foreign levy.** Macbeth fears both—malice domestic from Banquo and Macduff, foreign levy from the friends of Malcolm in England and of Donalbain in Ireland (3.1.30–33). 27. **Gentle my lord.** Since *my lord* is practically a single word, it is often preceded by an adjective.—**sleek o'er:** smooth over.—**rugged:** agitated; literally, rough, shaggy (3.4.100). Macbeth, being of an emotional temperament, has far less control over his features than his wife habitually exercises over hers. Cf. 2.5.58–63, 67.

Even after the murder, the Macbeths are equal partners, in love for most of the film (Morrisette, 2001).

MACB.	So shall I, love; and so, I pray, be you.	
	Let your remembrance apply to Banquo;	30
	Present him eminence both with eye and tongue—	
	Unsafe the while, that we	
	Must lave our honors in these flattering streams	
	And make our faces vizards to our hearts,	
	Disguising what they are.	
LADY.	You must leave this.	35
MACB.	O, full of scorpions is my mind, dear wife!	
	Thou know'st that Banquo, and his Fleance, lives.	
LADY.	But in them Nature's copy's not eterne.	
MACB.	There's comfort yet! They are assailable.	
	Then be thou jocund. Ere the bat hath flown	40

30. **Let...Banquo:** Remember to show particular attention to Banquo. *Apply to* means "to adapt one's self to a person," and hence "to be subservient or attentive to him," "to court his favor," or the like. 31. **Present him eminence:** do him special honor. 32. **Unsafe the while.** Macbeth interrupts himself with the bitter reflection that, while they are thus attentive to Banquo, they are themselves unsafe: the very necessity of flattering Banquo shows their fear of him. *Unsafe* refers to the persons mentioned in the preceding lines— "you and me."—**that:** in that, because. 33. **Must lave...streams:** must wash the honors that we have in streams of flattery to keep them clean. The thought is that, to retain their position, they must court the favor of Banquo and the rest. 34. **vizards:** masks. 35. **You must leave this:** such wild remarks and the mood that prompts them. Cf. 2.2.33–34: These deeds must not be thought / After these ways. So, it will make us mad. 38. **But...eterne:** Nature has granted them, not a perpetual lease of life but a mere copyhold tenure, easy to revoke or to terminate.

Their distance and formal postures show that Washizu (Macbeth) and Asaji (Lady Macbeth) begin to seperate emotionally even before the murders (Kurosawa, 1957).

His cloister'd flight, ere to black Hecate's summons
The shard-borne beetle with his drowsy hums
Hath rung night's yawning peal, there shall be done
A deed of dreadful note.

LADY.   What's to be done?

MACB.   Be innocent of the knowledge, dearest chuck,   45
Till thou applaud the deed. Come, seeling night,
Scarf up the tender eye of pitiful day,
And with thy bloody and invisible hand
Cancel and tear to pieces that great bond
Which keeps me pale. Light thickens, and the crow   50

41-43. **cloister'd.** The bat's flight is not, like a bird's, in the open air, but in belfries and cloisters—in darkness and solitude.—**ere...peal:** ere the droning beetle, in obedience to Hecate's summons, has announced the coming of drowsy night. Hecate, the goddess of darkness and of the deeds that befit it, issues the call for night to come, and the beetle rings the peal that publishes the summons to sleep. Here again (as in 2.1.52) Hecate is a goddess, not (as in the interpolated passages: 3.5, and 4.1.39–43) a mere witch.—**shard-borne:** borne upon wings that are like potsherds (fragments of pottery). The wing-cases of the beetle, which are elevated in flying, are commonly thought to be its wings. 44. **of dreadful note:** dreadful to be known.—**What's to be done?** The directness and concrete simplicity of Lady Macbeth's speeches are noteworthy; they accord with her strength of purpose and her habit of looking facts in the face. She finds that her husband no longer waits for her instigation, though he still requires comfort and encouragement from her. 45. The homely term of endearment (*chuck,* i.e., "chick") sounds grim in the savage context. The word was not grotesque, but merely familiar and affectionate. 46. **seeling night.** To *seel* is to sew up the eyelids (of a falcon) with silk—to keep it in the dark and tame it. 47. **Scarf up:** muffle (as with a scarf), blindfold. See Lady Macbeth's appeal to darkness (1.5.46–55) and cf. 2.1.49–56. 49. **bond:** the prophecy by which Fate has bound itself to give the throne to Banquo's descendants. 50. **thickens:** grows dim with the shades of night.

Makes wing to th' rooky wood.
Good things of day begin to droop and drowse,
Whiles night's black agents to their preys do rouse.
Thou marvell'st at my words; but hold thee still:
Things bad begun make strong themselves by ill.   55
So prithee go with me.   *Exeunt.*

SCENE III. [*Forres. A park near the Palace.*]

Enter three Murderers.

1. MUR.   But who did bid thee join with us?

3. MUR.   Macbeth.

2. MUR.   He needs not our mistrust, since he delivers
Our offices, and what we have to do,
To the direction just.

1. MUR.   Then stand with us.
The west yet glimmers with some streaks of day.   5
Now spurs the lated traveller apace
To gain the timely inn, and near approaches
The subject of our watch.

3. MUR.   Hark! I hear horses.

BAN.   (*within*) Give us a light there, ho!

2. MUR.   Then 'tis he! The rest

---

51. **th' rooky wood.** There were ravens about Macbeth's castle (cf. 1.5.34), and doubtless also rooks. A less probable interpretation makes *rooky* equivalent to the old adjective *roky*, "misty," "gloomy" (from *roke*, "smoke"; cf. *reek*). 52. **droop:** hang the head in sleep. 53. **agents:** all evil beings that act by night—beasts of prey, murderers, and the "spirits that tend on mortal thoughts" (1.5.36–37).
SCENE III.
1. We hear only the end of the dialogue. The Third Murderer has given the other two the information which Macbeth had promised to send them (3.1.128–131) and has proved that he is in the King's confidence by repeating such directions as they had already received. The identity of the Third Murderer has intrigued scholars, directors and readers for centuries. Seyton, Ross, Macbeth himself, and even one of the witches have been suggested. What is clear is that Macbeth is becoming increasingly distrustful, shutting out Lady Macbeth (cf 3.2.45) and hiring one murderer to make sure he is not betrayed by two others [A.C.]. 2-4. **delivers:** reports.—**offices:** duties.—**to the direction:** according to our instructions. 5. The time is carefully indicated. The sun has set, but there is a faint light in the west. When Banquo enters, however, it is dark enough for a torch. 6. **lated:** belated. 7. **To gain the timely inn:** to reach the inn in good season (before it is quite dark).—**near approaches.** This does not mean that he hears Banquo, but that the time is at hand when he is expected (cf. 3.1.129). 8. **subject:** object. 9. **Give...ho!** a call from Banquo to a servant of the palace who takes charge of the horses and gives the guests torches to light them as they walk up the avenue to the palace gate. Fleance takes the torch. Before Banquo and Fleance enter, they have entrusted their horses to the servant, and he has taken them out of sight. Thus the murderers are left alone with their victims.

	That are within the note of expectation	10
	Already are i' th' court.	
1. MUR.	His horses go about.	
3. MUR.	Almost a mile; but he does usually,	
	So all men do, from hence to th' palace gate	
	Make it their walk.	

Enter Banquo, *and* Fleance *with a torch.*

2. MUR.	A light, a light!	
3. MUR.	'Tis he.	
1. MUR.	Stand to't.	15
BAN.	It will be rain tonight.	
1. MUR.	Let it come down! [*They fall upon Banquo.*]	
BAN.	O, treachery! Fly, good Fleance, fly, fly, fly!	
	Thou mayst revenge. O slave! [*Dies. Fleance escapes.*]	
3. MUR.	Who did strike out the light?	
1. MUR.	Was't not the way?	
3. MUR.	There's but one down; the son is fled.	
2. MUR.	We have lost	20
	Best half of our affair.	
1. MUR.	Well, let's away, and say how much is done. *Exeunt.*	

SCENE IV. [*Forres. Hall in the Palace.*]

Banquet prepar'd. Enter Macbeth, Lady [Macbeth],
Ross, Lennox, Lords, *and* Attendants.

MACB.	You know your own degrees, sit down. At first
	And last the hearty welcome.
LORDS.	Thanks to your Majesty.

---

10. **within...expectation:** in the list of expected guests. 11. **His horses go about.** The speaker hears the servant galloping off with the horses. To attack and kill two active riders is not easy unless there are a large number of assailants. Hence Macbeth has arranged that the murder shall take place after Banquo and Fleance have dismounted. 16. **It will be rain tonight.** This casual remark about the weather is a master-stroke. It shows that Banquo is off his guard, and informs the audience that the night is cloudy and therefore fit for the murder. The savage jest of the murderer ("Let the storm come down, then!") fits the mood in which he commits the crime. He strikes Banquo with all the zest of revenge (cf. 3.1.85–91).

MACB.   Ourself will mingle with society
         And play the humble host.
         Our hostess keeps her state, but in best time   5
         We will require her welcome.

LADY.   Pronounce it for me, sir, to all our friends,
         For my heart speaks they are welcome.

                    Enter First Murderer [*to the door*].

MACB.   See, they encounter thee with their heart's thanks.
         Both sides are even. Here I'll sit i' th' midst.   10
         Be large in mirth; anon we'll drink a measure
         The table round. [*To first Murderer.*] There's blood upon thy face.

MUR.   'Tis Banquo's then.

MACB.   'Tis better thee without than he within.
         Is he dispatch'd?   15

MUR.   My lord, his throat is cut. That I did for him.

MACB.   Thou art the best o' th' cutthroats! Yet he's good
         That did the like for Fleance. If thou didst it,
         Thou art the nonpareil.

MUR.   Most royal sir,
         Fleance is scap'd.   20

MACB.   [*aside*] Then comes my fit again. I had else been perfect;
         Whole as the marble, founded as the rock,
         As broad and general as the casing air.
         But now I am cabin'd, cribb'd, confin'd, bound in
         To saucy doubts and fears.—But Banquo's safe?   25

MUR.   Ay, my good lord. Safe in a ditch he bides,
         With twenty trenched gashes on his head,
         The least a death to nature.

SCENE IV.
5–6. **keeps her state:** remains enthroned in her chair of state.—**in best time:** when the proper moment comes.—**require:** request, call for. 8. The first three speeches of the King and Queen each end with the word *welcome,* which is thus intentionally dwelt on. The Queen's word *heart* repeats her husband's *hearty* (line 2). 9. **encounter thee:** meet thee, respond to thee. 11. **large:** lavish, abundant.—**mirth:** enjoyment.—**a measure:** a large goblet, a bumper. 14. **'Tis…within:** It's better that the blood should be outside of thee than inside of Banquo. *He* for *him* is good seventeenth-century grammar. 21. **my fit:** my ague fit; my fit of feverous anxiety. Cf. 3.2.23. 22. **founded:** firmly established. 23. **broad and general:** free and unconfined.—**casing:** all-embracing. 24-25. **cabin'd, cribb'd:** shut up in a cabin—nay, in a mere hut.—**bound…fears:** shut in, with no companions but importunate doubts and fears (that force themselves upon me and will not let me alone).—**safe:** safely out of the way; disposed of. 27. **trenched:** deep-cut.

MACB.   Thanks for that.
There the grown serpent lies; the worm that's fled
Hath nature that in time will venom breed,   30
No teeth for th' present. Get thee gone. Tomorrow
We'll hear ourselves again.   *Exit Murderer.*

LADY.   My royal lord,
You do not give the cheer. The feast is sold
That is not often vouch'd, while 'tis a-making,
'Tis given with welcome. To feed were best at home.   35
From thence, the sauce to meat is ceremony;
Meeting were bare without it.

     Enter the Ghost of Banquo, *and sits in* Macbeth's *place.*†

MACB.   Sweet remembrancer!
Now good digestion wait on appetite,
And health on both!

LEN.   May't please your Highness sit.

MACB.   Here had we now our country's honor, roof'd,   40
Were the grac'd person of our Banquo present;
Who may I rather challenge for unkindness
Than pity for mischance.

ROSS.   His absence, sir,
Lays blame upon his promise. Please't your Highness
To grace us with your royal company?   45

---

29. **worm:** serpent. Cf. 3.2.13. 32. **hear ourselves:** talk with each other; confer. At the conference thus appointed the murderers may expect some reward, as promised in 3.1.106. 33–35. **give the cheer:** make your guests feel cordially welcome.—**The feast…welcome:** Unless the host's words and demeanor assure his guests that they are welcome, he might as well be an innkeeper.—**vouch'd:** certified.—**To feed:** to eat merely to satisfy hunger. 36. **From thence:** when away from home.—**meat:** food. 37. Banquo's ghost has been much discussed, some holding that it was an actual ghost, others that it was a figment of Macbeth's guilty conscience, like the air-drawn dagger to which Lady Macbeth compares it. A departed spirit (it was thought) might appear to one person in a company and remain invisible to the rest (cf. *Hamlet,* 3.4). In Shakespeare's theater (as the stage direction shows) Banquo's ghost entered and sat down in Macbeth's chair. This is proof positive that Shakespeare meant the audience to regard the ghost as actual; for how else could they regard it (in an age when belief in ghosts was universal) when they saw it with their own eyes? —**remembrancer:** one who reminds me of my duty. 38. **wait on:** attend. 40. **had we…roof'd:** we should now have all the noblest men of Scotland under one roof. 41. **grac'd:** honored, noble. 42-43. **Who may I…mischance!** whom I hope I should rather blame for unkindness (in staying away on purpose) than pity for some accident (that has prevented his coming). 45. **grace:** honor.

---

†   Directors have shown the Ghost in a variety of ways. Welles shows both the empty and the taken chair, making the Ghost as much a hallucination as the dagger. Kurosawa's victim sits unmoving, ignoring Washizu, and recognizable as a corpse only by his unbound hair. In contrast, in *Men of Respect,* the Ghost of Bankie staggers through the picnic covered in blood and pointing directly at Macbeth in accusation. [A.C.]

MACB.	The table's full.
LEN.	Here is a place reserv'd, sir.
MACB.	Where?
LEN.	Here, my good lord. What is't that moves your Highness?
MACB.	Which of you have done this?
LORDS.	What, my good lord?

MACB.   Thou canst not say I did it. Never shake   50
Thy gory locks at me.

ROSS.   Gentlemen, rise. His Highness is not well.

LADY.   Sit, worthy friends. My lord is often thus,
And hath been from his youth. Pray you keep seat.
The fit is momentary; upon a thought   55
He will again be well. If much you note him,
You shall offend him and extend his passion.
Feed, and regard him not.—Are you a man?

MACB.   Ay, and a bold one, that dare look on that
Which might appal the devil.

LADY.   O proper stuff!   60
This is the very painting of your fear.
This is the air-drawn dagger which you said
Led you to Duncan. O, these flaws and starts
(Impostors to true fear) would well become
A woman's story at a winter's fire,   65
Authoriz'd by her grandam. Shame itself!
Why do you make such faces? When all's done,
You look but on a stool.

MACB.   Prithee see there! behold! look! lo! How say you?
Why, what care I? If thou canst nod, speak too.   70

---

48. **moves:** disturbs. 49. **Which of you have done this?** Two interpretations are manifestly possible: (1) "Which of you has killed Banquo?" (2) "Which of you has set this corpse in my chair?" That the first is correct is shown by Macbeth's words in line 50: "Thou canst not say I did it." To the astonished guests Macbeth's question is inexplicable. 51. **gory locks.** The long hair of the apparition is matted with blood from the "twenty trenched gashes." Cf. 4.1.113, 123. 55. **upon a thought:** in a moment. 57. **shall:** will surely; will be sure to.—**offend him:** make him worse.—**passion:** attack. 58. **Are you a man?** Cf. 1.7.46–51. 60. **O proper stuff!** A fine thing this! 62. **air-drawn:** unsheathed and floating in the air—with a contemptuous implication of unreality, as if drawn (delineated) by the air. 63. **Led.** Cf. 2.1.42: "Thou marshall'st me the way that I was going."—**flaws:** outbursts—from the sense of "a sudden gust of wind."—**starts:** nervous movements. 64. **to:** in comparison with. These are mere tricks of the nerves, unworthy to be called genuine fear. They are like the shudders with which children listen to a ghost story, safely gathered round the cottage fire. 66. **Authóriz'd:** vouched for. The woman who tells the old wife's tale can cite only her grandmother as authority. 67. **Why...faces?** Here again Lady Macbeth chides her husband for not being able to control his countenance.

	If charnel houses and our graves must send
	Those that we bury back, our monuments
	Shall be the maws of kites. [*Exit Ghost.*]
LADY.	What, quite unmann'd in folly?
MACB.	If I stand here, I saw him.
LADY.	Fie, for shame!

MACB. Blood hath been shed ere now, i' th' olden time, 75
Ere humane statute purg'd the gentle weal;
Ay, and since too, murders have been perform'd
Too terrible for the ear. The time has been
That, when the brains were out, the man would die,
And there an end! But now they rise again, 80
With twenty mortal murders on their crowns,
And push us from our stools. This is more strange
Than such a murder is.

LADY. My worthy lord,
Your noble friends do lack you.

MACB. I do forget.
Do not muse at me, my most worthy friends. 85
I have a strange infirmity, which is nothing
To those that know me. Come, love and health to all!
Then I'll sit down. Give me some wine, fill full.

Enter Ghost.

I drink to th' general joy o' th' whole table,
And to our dear friend Banquo, whom we miss. 90
Would he were here! To all, and him, we thirst,
And all to all.

LORDS. Our duties, and the pledge.

MACB. Avaunt, and quit my sight! Let the earth hide thee!
Thy bones are marrowless, thy blood is cold;

---

71. **charnel houses.** A charnel house was a vault or small building attached to a church and used as a storehouse for such skulls and bones as came to light in digging new graves. 72-73. **our monuments... kites:** the dead shall be thrown out in the open fields to be devoured by birds of prey, and thus the only monuments we allow them shall be the bellies of kites. Then, perhaps, they will not come back to haunt us. 76. **Ere...weal:** before civilizing law cleansed society (of primeval savagery) and made it gentle (i.e., in the old times of lawless barbarism). 77. **since too:** even under the reign of law and order (as opposed to primeval anarchy). 81. **twenty...crowns.** An echo of the murderer's words in lines 27–28.—**mortal murders:** murderous wounds. 83. **worthy:** noble. 84. **lack you:** miss your company. 85. **muse:** wonder, be astonished. —**To all...thirst:** I am eager to drink to you all, and to Banquo in particular. 92. **And all to all:** and let everybody drink to everybody. The toast is to be a general health. —**Our duties, and the pledge:** Our toast is—homage to your Majesty, and a health to the whole table and to Banquo.

| | Thou hast no speculation in those eyes | 95 |
| | Which thou dost glare with! | |

LADY.   Think of this, good peers,
But as a thing of custom. 'Tis no other.
Only it spoils the pleasure of the time.

MACB.   What man dare, I dare.
Approach thou like the rugged Russian bear,   100
The arm'd rhinoceros, or th' Hyrcan tiger;
Take any shape but that, and my firm nerves
Shall never tremble. Or be alive again
And dare me to the desert with thy sword.
If trembling I inhabit then, protest me   105
The baby of a girl. Hence, horrible shadow!
Unreal mock'ry, hence!   [*Exit Ghost.*]
                         Why, so! Being gone,
I am a man again. Pray you sit still.

LADY.   You have displac'd the mirth, broke the good meeting
With most admir'd disorder.

MACB.   Can such things be,   110
And overcome us like a summer's cloud
Without our special wonder? You make me strange
Even to the disposition that I owe,
When now I think you can behold such sights
And keep the natural ruby of your cheeks   115
When mine is blanch'd with fear.

ROSS.   What sights, my lord?

---

95. **speculation:** intelligent sight. The ghost's eyes are like a dead man's—fixed in a glassy stare. 97. **no other:** nothing else. 99. **What man dare, I dare:** an echo of 1.7.46: "I dare do all that may become a man." 100. **like:** in the shape of. —**rugged:** shaggy and fierce. Cf. 3.2.27.—**Russian:** bears were imported from Russia for the bear-baiting at Paris Garden. 101-102. **arm'd:** arm-clad, armored.—**nerves:** sinews. 104. **to the desert:** to some solitary place, for a duel to the death without seconds or witnesses. 105. **If trembling I inhabit then:** If then, as now, I live in terror. *Trembling* is a participle and *inhabit* means "live and move and have my being." 106. **The baby of a girl:** the child of a very young mother—and so, "a timid weakling." 107. **Unreal mock'ry.** Macbeth tries hard to believe that the ghost is a creature of his imagination, and the closing lines of the scene show that, with his wife's help, he succeeds. But he knows better in the long run, and later he refers to the spectre as indeed "the spirit of Banquo" (4.1.112).—**mock'ry:** illusion.—**so!** very well!—**Being gone:** now that it is gone. 110. **With most admir'd disorder:** by an amazing fit of distraction. 111-112. **overcome...wonder?** come over us as suddenly as a cloud in summer, and yet excite no more surprise than such a cloud? 112-113. **You...owe:** You make me feel that I do not know my own nature, which I had supposed to be that of a brave man.—**disposition:** mental and moral make-up or constitution.—**owe:** own. 116. **mine:** the natural ruby of *my* cheeks.

LADY.   I pray you speak not. He grows worse and worse;
          Question enrages him. At once, good night.
          Stand not upon the order of your going,
          But go at once.

LEN.   Good night, and better health   120
          Attend his Majesty!

LADY.   A kind good night to all!

                                        Exeunt Lords [and Attendants].

MACB.   It will have blood, they say; blood will have blood.
          Stones have been known to move and trees to speak;
          Augures and understood relations have
          By maggot-pies and choughs and rooks brought forth   125
          The secret'st man of blood. What is the night?

LADY.   Almost at odds with morning, which is which.

MACB.   How say'st thou that Macduff denies his person
          At our great bidding?

LADY.   Did you send to him, sir?

MACB.   I hear it by the way; but I will send.   130
          There's not a one of them but in his house
          I keep a servant fee'd. I will tomorrow
          (And betimes I will) unto the Weird Sisters.

---

118. **enrages:** drives into a frenzy.—**At once, good night:** I bid you all a hasty good-night in a body, without waiting to take ceremonious leave of each in turn. 119. **Stand...going:** Do not be punctilious about precedence as you leave the hall. Under ordinary circumstances the nobles would depart slowly and ceremoniously, in the order of their rank. 123-126. **Stones...blood.** Macbeth recalls various instances in which murders have been miraculously brought to light. The theory was that murder is so atrocious in God's eyes that he will not suffer it to go undetected. 123. **Stones have been known to move:** so as to reveal the body that the murderer had hidden.—**trees to speak:** as in the case of the murdered Polydorus in the Aeneid, 3.19–68. 124. **Augures:** auguries, signs from the flight of birds.—**understood relations:** reports properly comprehended. The appearance and flight of the birds give the *relation* or *report,* but this must be interpreted by a person skilled in augury before it can be understood. *Relation* almost always means "report or recital" in Shakespeare (cf. 4.3.173). 125. **By:** by means of.—**maggot-pies:** magpies.—**choughs:** a kind of crow.—**rooks.** Cf. 3.2.51.—**brought forth:** revealed, brought to light. 126. **What is the night?** What time of night is it? 127. **at odds:** at variance, disputing. It is, then, about midnight. Thus this scene accounts for several hours of dramatic time. 128. **How say'st thou that...?** What do you say to the fact that...? From her reply it appears that Lady Macbeth has not heard of Macduff's refusal to come to court. 130. **by the way:** incidentally; in the ordinary course of affairs. Macbeth explains that the report has come from one of Macduff's household who is the King's spy. Macduff had avoided attending the coronation (2.4.36) and has remained on his estates at Fife ever since. He has never positively refused a royal summons, but the spy has heard him declare that he means to stay away from court. His absence from the "solemn supper" confirms Macbeth's suspicions of his hostility. 131-132. **There's not...fee'd.** Macbeth's statement that he keeps a paid spy in the house of every one of the Scottish nobles is an indication of his growing paranoia [A.C.]. 133. **betimes:** soon, without delay.

More shall they speak; for now I am bent to know
By the worst means the worst. For mine own good   135
All causes shall give way. I am in blood
Stepp'd in so far that, should I wade no more,
Returning were as tedious as go o'er.
Strange things I have in head, that will to hand,
Which must be acted ere they may be scann'd   140

LADY.   You lack the season of all natures, sleep.

MACB.   Come, we'll to sleep. My strange and self-abuse
Is the initiate fear that wants hard use.
We are yet but young in deed.   *Exeunt.*

SCENE V. [*A heath.*]†

Thunder. Enter the three Witches, *meeting* Hecate.

1. WITCH.   Why, how now, Hecate? You look angerly.

HEC.   Have I not reason, beldams as you are,
Saucy and overbold? How did you dare
To trade and traffic with Macbeth
In riddles and affairs of death;   5
And I, the mistress of your charms,
The close contriver of all harms,
Was never call'd to bear my part
Or show the glory of our art?

---

134. **More shall they speak.** An echo of what Macbeth says on the first appearance of the Sisters: "Stay, you imperfect speakers, tell me more!" (1.3.70).—**bent:** determined. 135. **By the worst means:** i.e., *even* by the worst means. Macbeth no longer doubts that the Weird Sisters are powers of evil (cf. 1.3.130–137). 136. **All causes:** all considerations. These include the scruples he would ordinarily have felt about seeking the help of the infernal powers. 139. **will to hand:** are bound to be executed. 140. **ere...scann'd:** before I pause to consider them. 141. **the season:** the preservative; that without which no living creature can remain sound and normal. The emphasis on sleep in 3.2.16 ff., and in the present scene is deeply significant. It looks back to the prophecy of the voice that cried "Sleep no more!" (2.2.35–43) and forward to the sleepwalking scene (5.1). 142. **My strange and self-abuse:** my strange self-deception. 143. **the initiate fear:** fear felt by a novice (one just initiated in crime).—**wants:** lacks.—**hard use:** practice that hardens one.

SCENE V.
1-2. **angerly:** angrily.—**beldams:** hags. 7. **close:** secret.—**of all harms:** of all the evil deeds you do.

---

†   This scene is accepted as an interpolation, added by someone other than Shakespeare. Interestingly, despite the generally accepted belief that it is not Shakespeare's work, all editions (including this one) include the scene. On the other hand, very few productions do. After the middle of the nineteenth century, when Shakespeare's text was returned to the stage (see introduction), directors almost universally cut this scene, so those who do include it, such as Peter Hall in 1967, feel the need to defend their decision. [A.C.]

And, which is worse, all you have done   10
Hath been but for a wayward sun,
Spiteful and wrathful, who, as others do,
Loves for his own ends, not for you.
But make amends now. Get you gone
And at the pit of Acheron   15
Meet me i' th' morning. Thither he
Will come to know his destiny.
Your vessels and your spells provide,
Your charms and everything beside.
I am for th' air. This night I'll spend   20
Unto a dismal and a fatal end.
Great business must be wrought ere noon.
Upon the corner of the moon
There hangs a vap'rous drop profound.
I'll catch it ere it come to ground;   25
And that, distill'd by magic sleights,
Shall raise such artificial sprites
As by the strength of their illusion
Shall draw him on to his confusion.
He shall spurn fate, scorn death, and bear   30
His hopes 'bove wisdom, grace, and fear;
And you all know security
Is mortals' chiefest enemy.

                              Music and a song within.
                    "Come away, come away," &c.

Hark! I am call'd. My little spirit, see,
Sits in a foggy cloud and stays for me.   [*Exit.*] 35

1. WITCH.   Come, let's make haste. She'll soon be back again.   *Exeunt.*

---

12. **Spiteful and wrathful.** This has no pertinence. Macbeth has had no relations of any kind with the Sisters since their first meeting in 1.3. 13. **Loves.** Again a false note. Macbeth has never professed to love the Sisters or to be a devotee of art magic. 15. **the pit of Acheron.** a river of the infernal regions. 21. **dismal:** disastrous. **a vap'rous drop profound:** a drop of condensed vapor, deep-hanging, pear-shaped, and so about to fall. The allusion is, like Acheron, rather out of place in Scottish wizardry. When we come to the scene in the cavern (4.1), this moon-vapor is nowhere mentioned among the ingredients of the cauldron, though Hecate here regards it as of prime importance. 26. **sleights:** secret arts. 27. **artificial sprites:** spirits produced by art magic. 29. **confusion:** destruction, ruin. 31. **grace:** goodness, virtue. 32. **security:** overweening confidence. 33. **song.** The song (from Middleton's tragicomedy of *The Witch*) is included in the 1673 Quarto of *Macbeth* and in Davenant's adaptation. Perhaps only the first two lines are to be sung here: "Come away! come away! / Hecate, Hecate, come away!"

Scene VI. [*Forres. The Palace.*]

Enter Lennox *and another* Lord.

Len.	My former speeches have but hit your thoughts,
	Which can interpret farther. Only I say
	Things have been strangely borne. The gracious Duncan
	Was pitied of Macbeth. Marry, he was dead!
	And the right valiant Banquo walk'd too late;
	Whom, you may say (if't please you) Fleance kill'd,
	For Fleance fled. Men must not walk too late.
	Who cannot want the thought how monstrous
	It was for Malcolm and for Donalbain
	To kill their gracious father? Damned fact!
	How it did grieve Macbeth! Did he not straight,
	In pious rage, the two delinquents tear,
	That were the slaves of drink and thralls of sleep?
	Was not that nobly done? Ay, and wisely too.
	For 'twould have anger'd any heart alive
	To hear the men deny't. So that I say
	He has borne all things well; and I do think
	That, had he Duncan's sons under his key
	(As, an't please heaven, he shall not), they should find
	What 'twere to kill a father. So should Fleance.
	But peace, for from broad words, and 'cause he fail'd
	His presence at the tyrant's feast, I hear
	Macduff lives in disgrace. Sir, can you tell

Line numbers: 5, 10, 15, 20

Scene VI.

In the interval, short as it is, between scene 4 and scene 6 Macbeth has carried out his purpose of summoning Macduff (3.4.130), and the messenger has returned with a curt refusal. Macduff has fled and is on his way to England. Contrast Lennox's state of mind immediately after the murder of Duncan (2.3.91–96). 1. **My former speeches.** Lennox has been telling what happened at the banquet.—**hit your thoughts:** agreed with what you had been thinking. 2. **Which...farther:** Your mind can easily draw its own conclusions from the hints I have given.—**Only:** All I have to say is—. 3. **strangely borne:** oddly managed by Macbeth. Cf. line 17. What follows in lines 3–20 is in a strain of studied irony. 4. **of:** by.—**Marry:** an oath, "by the Virgin Mary"; but often used lightly, as here, where it means simply "to be sure." 7. **Men must not walk too late.** Profoundly ironical. In Scotland, as things are now, it is not safe for anybody whom Macbeth dislikes to be out after dark! 8. **Who cannot want the thought?** Who can help thinking? This is simply an instance of the double negative: *cannot want* for *can want*. 10. **fact:** evil deed, crime. 11. **Did he not straight,** etc. Macbeth's hasty act is ironically ascribed to indignation at the enormity of the crime, but his real motive is plainly hinted in line 16—to get the chamberlains out of the way before they could protest their innocence.—**straight:** straightway, immediately. 12. **pious rage:** a frenzy of loyalty. *Pious* often describes the filial affection of children or the loyal devotion of subjects.—**delinquents:** offenders. 13. **the slaves of drink.** Lennox insinuates that the chamberlains could not have killed Duncan, for they had slept the sleep of drunkenness all night long. 19. **an:** if.—**should find:** would certainly find; would be sure to find. 20. **So should Fleance.** This repeats, with condensed ironic power, the argument of lines 6–7. The implication is that Malcolm and Donalbain are just as innocent as Fleance. 21. **from broad words:** because of too free or unguarded expressions. These have been reported to Macbeth by a spy (see 3.4.128–132). 22. **tyrant's:** usurper's.

Where he bestows himself?

LORD.   The son of Duncan,
From whom this tyrant holds the due of birth,   25
Lives in the English court, and is receiv'd
Of the most pious Edward with such grace
That the malevolence of fortune nothing
Takes from his high respect. Thither Macduff
Is gone to pray the holy King upon his aid   30
To wake Northumberland and warlike Siward;
That by the help of these (with Him above
To ratify the work) we may again
Give to our tables meat, sleep to our nights,
Free from our feasts and banquets bloody knives,   35
Do faithful homage and receive free honors—
All which we pine for now. And this report
Hath so exasperate the King that he
Prepares for some attempt of war.

LEN.   Sent he to Macduff?

LORD.   He did; and with an absolute "Sir, not I!"   40
The cloudy messenger turns me his back
And hums, as who should say, "You'll rue the time
That clogs me with this answer."

LEN.   And that well might
Advise him to a caution t' hold what distance
His wisdom can provide. Some holy angel   45
Fly to the court of England and unfold
His message ere he come, that a swift blessing
May soon return to this our suffering country
Under a hand accurs'd!

LORD.   I'll send my prayers with him.   *Exeunt.*

---

24. **bestows himself:** has taken refuge. Cf. 3.1.30–31. 25. **holds:** withholds.—**due of birth:** birthright. 27. **Of:** by.—**Edward:** Edward the Confessor, who reigned from 1042 to 1066 (see 4.3.140–159).—**grace:** favor. 29. **his high respect:** the high regard in which he is held. 30. **upon his aid:** for his assistance. 31. **wake:** call to arms.—**Northumberland:** i.e., the people of that region.—**Siward:** Earl of Northumberland. 34. **meat:** food. 36. **faithful:** sincere.—**free:** unconstrained; i.e., granted with good will on the King's part. At present their homage to Macbeth is insincere, and the honor that he shows them in return is not voluntary (free), because it is the result of fear. Cf. what Macbeth says in 3.2.32–35. 37. **this report:** the report of the favor with which Malcolm is treated. Macbeth fears an invasion. Cf. 3.1.30–33. 38. **exasperate:** exasperated. 40. **He did.** This refers, not to an invitation to the supper, but to a summons sent since (see 3.4.130). 41. **cloudy:** frowning, gloomy. The messenger looks gloomy because he is reluctant to carry such unwelcome tidings to a man of Macbeth's temper. Compare Macbeth's treatment of the person who reports the approach of Birnam Wood (5.5.35–40). 42. **hums.** This indicates a surly murmuring sound.—**as who should say:** as if he were saying; as if to say. 43. **clogs me:** makes me return with reluctant feet. 46. **unfold:** disclose, reveal. 48–49. **our...accurs'd:** our country, suffering under, etc. A common order.

One of the ways in which Kurosawa (1957) adapted *Macbeth* was to use this singular forest spirit, endlessly spinning, rather than three Weird Sisters.

ACT IV

SCENE I. [*A cavern. In the middle, a cauldron boiling.*]

Thunder. Enter the three Witches.

1. WITCH.	Thrice the brinded cat hath mew'd.	
2. WITCH.	Thrice and once the hedge-pig whin'd.	
3. WITCH.	Harpier cries; 'tis time, 'tis time.	
1. WITCH.	Round about the cauldron go;	
	In the poison'd entrails throw.	5
	Toad, that under cold stone	
	Days and nights has thirty-one	
	Swelt'red venom sleeping got,	
	Boil thou first i' th' charmed pot.	
ALL.	Double, double, toil and trouble;	10
	Fire burn, and cauldron bubble.	

ACT IV. SCENE I.

There is no indication of place in the Folios except "Open locks, Whoever knocks" (lines 46, 47). Most editors lay the scene in a cavern. An old ruin in a desolate region would do as well. 1–3. **brinded:** brindled, striped. The cat, the hedgehog, and Harpier are familiar (i.e., attendant) spirits, like Graymalkin and Paddock in 1.1. *Harpier* is a proper name formed, apparently, from *harpy.*—**'tis time.** Some editors make Harpier say this. 8. **Swelt'red:** coming out in drops, like sweat.

Morrissette (2001) presents humorous hippies instead of witches, but only Macbeth ever sees them, and then only when very drunk, suggesting they don't actually exist.

2. WITCH.	Fillet of a fenny snake,
	In the cauldron boil and bake;
	Eye of newt, and toe of frog,
	Wool of bat, and tongue of dog, 15
	Adder's fork, and blindworm's sting,
	Lizard's leg, and howlet's wing;
	For a charm of pow'rful trouble
	Like a hell-broth boil and bubble.
ALL.	Double, double, toil and trouble; 20
	Fire burn, and cauldron bubble.
3. WITCH.	Scale of dragon, tooth of wolf
	Witch's mummy, maw and gulf
	Of the ravin'd salt-sea shark,
	Root of hemlock, digg'd i' th' dark; 25
	Liver of blaspheming Jew,
	Gall of goat, and slips of yew

---

12. **Fillet:** slice. 16. The blindworm (or slowworm) is a small snake-like lizard erroneously supposed to be sightless. Though not in fact venomous, it is still popularly regarded as dangerous. 17. **howlet:** owlet. 23. **Witch's mummy:** mummified fragment of a witch. Human flesh was thought to be powerful in magic—especially the flesh of criminals, of non-Christians, or of persons who had met with a violent death or had not had Christian burial.—**maw and gulf:** stomach and gullet. 24. **ravin'd:** ravenous. Formed from the noun *ravin* or *raven* (Lat. *rapina*), "voracity," by means of the suffix *-ed* (meaning "provided with," or "characterized by"). Beasts of prey were often called "beasts of ravin." 25. **i' th' dark.** The time when an herb was gathered was supposed to affect its potency in medicine (cf. line 28). 27. **yew:** a graveyard tree thought to be poisonous.

Sliver'd in the moon's eclipse;
Nose of Turk and Tartar's lips;
Finger of birth-strangled babe   30
Ditch-deliver'd by a drab:
Make the gruel thick and slab.
Add thereto a tiger's chaudron
For th' ingredience of our cauldron.

ALL.   Double, double, toil and trouble;   35
            Fire burn, and cauldron bubble.

2. WITCH.   Cool it with a baboon's blood,
            Then the charm is firm and good.

                    Enter Hecate *to the other three* Witches.

HEC.   O, well done! I commend your pains,
            And every one shall share i' th' gains.   40
            And now about the cauldron sing
            Like elves and fairies in a ring,
            Enchanting all that you put in.

                                        Music and a song,
                    "Black spirits," &c.   [*Exit Hecate.*]

2. WITCH.   By the pricking of my thumbs,
            Something wicked this way comes.   45
                Open locks,
                Whoever knocks!

                    Enter Macbeth.

MACB.   How now, you secret, black, and midnight hags?
            What is't you do?

---

28. **eclipse:** a particularly ill-omened time. 30. **birth-strangled:** strangled as soon as born, and hence not baptized. Infants who died unchristened were the object of many superstitions. Sometimes they were thought to haunt the earth as a kind of demon. In any case, their flesh was regarded as powerful in evil spells. 31. **Ditch-deliver'd:** born in a ditch.—**drab:** harlot, whore. 32. **gruel.** A bit of savage grotesqueness, like 'hell-broth.'—**slab:** thick, viscous. 33. **chaudron:** liver and lights. 34. **ingredience:** composition. Cf. 1.7.11. *Cauldron* rhymes with *chaudron.* 39–43. Hecate's speech is in an iambic metre (the same that she uses in 3.5), very different in its effect from the trochaic metre that precedes, and is obviously by the same hand as 3.5. She does not bring the lunar venom which she mentioned as to be used in "raising artificial sprites." There are other contradictions. The mention of "gains" is one, for there are no gains: the Sisters expect nothing from Macbeth; they disappear without waiting for a reward. The comparison with elves and fairies is quite out of tune. Line 43 makes no sense, for all the ingredients have already been "put in," the charm is already "firm and good," and the incantation has been finished in line 38 (cf. 1.3.37). 43. **Black spirits.** This song, of which the Folios give only the first two words, is doubtless by Middleton, in whose tragicomedy of *The Witch* it occurs. It is inserted (obviously from *The Witch*) in Davenant's version of *Macbeth.* 44. **pricking:** an old sign of the approach of some evil person or some strange event. 46. **Open locks.** This does not imply that the Sisters are in a locked room rather than a cave. It is a formula of admission, releasing any spells that prevent the entrance of intruders.

ALL.   A deed without a name.

MACB.   I conjure you by that which you profess   50
                 (Howe'er you come to know it), answer me.
                 Though you untie the winds and let them fight
                 Against the churches; though the yesty waves
                 Confound and swallow navigation up;
                 Though bladed corn be lodg'd and trees blown down;   55
                 Though castles topple on their warders' heads;
                 Though palaces and pyramids do slope
                 Their heads to their foundations; though the treasure
                 Of nature's germens tumble all together,
                 Even till destruction sicken—answer me   60
                 To what I ask you.

1. WITCH.   Speak.

2. WITCH.   Demand.

3. WITCH.   We'll answer.

1. WITCH.   Say, if th' hadst rather hear it from our mouths
                 Or from our masters.

MACB.   Call 'em! Let me see 'em.

1. WITCH.   Pour in sow's blood, that hath eaten
                 Her nine farrow; grease that's sweaten   65
                 From the murderer's gibbet throw
                 Into the flame.

ALL.   Come, high or low;

---

50. **cónjure:** call upon solemnly.—**by...profess:** i.e., the prophetic power which, as their words to him and Banquo had implied, they profess to have (1.3.48 ff.). 51. **Howe'er...it:** no matter if your knowledge comes from infernal sources. He is determined to know "by the worst means the worst" (3.4.135). **Though you untie,** etc.: Though the evil spells which you must use are so powerful as to bring utter ruin upon the whole earth, yet I will have you reveal the future to me. Cf. 3.2.16–19.—**untie the winds:** an allusion to the power which witches (especially those of the North) were believed to exercise over wind and weather (cf. 1.3.11 ff.). 53. **yesty:** yeasty, foaming. 54. **Confound:** destroy. 55. **bladed corn.** If wheat in the blade is lodged (beaten down flat by wind and rain), the crop fails and famine ensues. 56. **topple:** fall in ruins. 57. **slope:** let fall. 58-59. **the treasure...germens:** the accumulated store of those elemental seeds or germs from which everything in the future is to spring. This is equivalent to saying, "though the orderly universe be destroyed and chaos come again." For the metaphor cf. "the seeds of time" in 1.3.58. 60. **sicken:** is satiated, and sickens at its own work. 61. **Demand:** ask. 62-63. **Say...masters.** The Weird Sisters give Macbeth his choice between visions and mere prophecy.—**Call 'em! Let me see 'em.** The bare colloquial simplicity of these words, as contrasted with the solemn adjuration of Macbeth's preceding speech, produces an effect of fierce intensity of purpose. He wishes to know the truth and is determined to get it at first hand. 65. **farrow:** young pigs. For the mystic *nine,* cf. 1.3.36.—**grease.** The flame is made to flare up by adding the fat of a murderer.—**sweaten:** sweated. 67. **high or low:** wherever thou art, whether in the upper or lower air, under the earth, or in hell. This is much better than to interpret *high or low* as "spirits of high or low degree"; for no "weak masters" are now invoked, and, besides, the summons is to one spirit only, as "thyself" shows.

Thyself and office deftly show!

Thunder. First Apparition, an Armed Head.[†]

MACB. Tell me, thou unknown power—

1. WITCH.   He knows thy thought.
Hear his speech, but say thou naught.   70

1. APPAR. Macbeth! Macbeth! Macbeth! Beware Macduff;
Beware the Thane of Fife. Dismiss me. Enough.   *He descends.*

MACB. Whate'er thou art, for thy good caution thanks!
Thou hast harp'd my fear aright. But one word more—

1. WITCH. He will not be commanded. Here's another,   75
More potent than the first.

Thunder. Second Apparition, a Bloody Child.

2. APPAR. Macbeth! Macbeth! Macbeth!

MACB. Had I three ears, I'd hear thee.

2. APPAR. Be bloody, bold, and resolute; laugh to scorn
The pow'r of man, for none of woman born   80
Shall harm Macbeth.   *Descends.*

MACB. Then live, Macduff. What need I fear of thee?
But yet I'll make assurance double sure
And take a bond of fate. Thou shalt not live.
That I may tell pale-hearted fear it lies   85
And sleep in spite of thunder.

---

68. **office:** function.—**deftly:** skilfully.—**an Armed Head.** This typifies Macduff as he is known to Macbeth—i.e., as a warrior who may return to fight against the tyrant. The speech of the apparition tells nothing that Macbeth does not already know: it merely expresses the fear that haunts his mind. The first apparition, then, is parallel to the greeting of the First Sister, "Hail to thee, Thane of Glamis!" (1.3.48). 70. **Hear...naught.** The powers which the Sisters have evoked are so tremendous that they themselves stand in awe of them (cf. line 89). 74. **harp'd my fear aright:** sounded it forth on the right string (expressed it truly).—**But one word more.** Cf. 1.3.70. 76. The Second Apparition represents Macduff, but Macduff in a character in which he is unknown to Macbeth until the end of the play—i.e., as not born of woman. Thus this apparition and his prophecy accord with the greeting of the Second Witch, "Hail to thee, Thane of Cawdor!" (1.3.49). They stand for something which is true at the moment but unknown to Macbeth.—**More potent.** Macduff, as the man not born of woman, and therefore the fated agent of Macbeth's destruction, is more potent than Macduff as a mere human enemy. 84. **take a bond of fate.** Fate has given its word that none born of woman shall harm Macbeth, but he is not satisfied with Fate's *word*—he requires a *bond*. 86. **a Child Crowned,** etc. The Third Apparition typifies Malcolm as king and the advance of his soldiers with branches of Birnam Wood in their hands.

[†]   Film directors have offered a vast range of approaches to this scene. Polanski has Macbeth enter a trance-like hallucination, where he is warned of Macduff by a doppelganger rather than a bloody head. In *Scotland PA* and *Men of Respect* there are no visions, but apparent possession of the main witch by spirits, who speak the warnings through her. Stage productions have used film, marionettes and lighting to suggest that the power of the witches both is and is not real.

Thunder. Third Apparition, a Child Crowned, with a tree in his hand.

What is this

      That rises like the issue of a king
      And wears upon his baby-brow the round
      And top of sovereignty?

ALL.   Listen, but speak not to't.

3. APPAR.   Be lion-mettled, proud, and take no care   90
      Who chafes, who frets, or where conspirers are.
      Macbeth shall never vanquish'd be until
      Great Birnam Wood to high Dunsinane Hill
      Shall come against him.   *Descends.*

MACB.   That will never be.
      Who can impress the forest, bid the tree   95
      Unfix his earth-bound root? Sweet bodements, good!
      Rebellion's head rise never till the Wood
      Of Birnam rise, and our high-plac'd Macbeth
      Shall live the lease of nature, pay his breath
      To time and mortal custom. Yet my heart   100
      Throbs to know one thing. Tell me, if your art
      Can tell so much—shall Banquo's issue ever
      Reign in this kingdom?

ALL.   Seek to know no more.

MACB.   I will be satisfied. Deny me this,
      And an eternal curse fall on you! Let me know.   105
      Why sinks that cauldron? and what noise is this?

                                       Hautboys.

1. WITCH.   Show!

2. WITCH.   Show!

3. WITCH.   Show!

---

87. **like:** in the shape of. 88. **round:** Cf. 1.5.24: "the golden round." 89. **top:** diadem.—**speak not.** Cf. line 70. 91. **chafes:** is resentful or discontented. 93. **Dunsínane.** The Moving Wood is a widespread incident in folklore and saga. 94. **That will never be.** Macbeth, in eager acceptance of the oracle, continues it in the same rhymed form. In effect, he makes himself his own prophet: he identifies himself, as it were, with the lying spirits whom he has consulted, and whom he trusts to the end. Thus *our* in line 98 is in perfect keeping (as if the speaker were still the apparition, not Macbeth himself). 95. **impress:** enlist forcibly; press into service. 96. **bodements:** prophecies. 99. **live the lease of nature:** live the allotted term of his natural life and die a natural death. Cf. 3.2.38: "Nature's copy." 100. **mortal custom:** the custom of dying, which is common to all men. 104. **I will be satisfied:** I am determined to have full information. 106. **noise:** common in the sense of "music." 106. **Hautboys:** Early form of the oboe (a musical cue). [A.C.]

| ALL. | Show his eyes, and grieve his heart! | 110 |
| | Come like shadows, so depart! | |

A show of eight Kings, [the eighth] with a glass in his hand, and Banquo last.

MACB.	Thou art too like the spirit of Banquo. Down!	
	Thy crown does sear mine eyeballs. And thy hair,	
	Thou other gold-bound brow, is like the first.	
	A third is like the former. Filthy hags!	115
	Why do you show me this? A fourth? Start, eyes!	
	What, will the line stretch out to th' crack of doom?	
	Another yet? A seventh? I'll see no more.	
	And yet the eighth appears, who bears a glass	
	Which shows me many more; and some I see	120
	That twofold balls and treble sceptres carry.	
	Horrible sight! Now I see 'tis true;	
	For the blood-bolter'd Banquo smiles upon me	
	And points at them for his. [*Apparitions vanish.*] What? Is this so?	

1. WITCH.	Ay, sir, all this is so. But why	125
	Stands Macbeth thus amazedly?	
	Come, sisters, cheer we up his sprites	
	And show the best of our delights.	
	I'll charm the air to give a sound	
	While you perform your antic round,	130
	That this great king may kindly say	
	Our duties did his welcome pay.	

Music. The Witches dance, and vanish.

---

111. **A show:** i.e., a dumb show; an exhibition of actors that do not speak. 112. **Thou…Banquo.** Said to the first of the Eight Kings. Banquo himself is not seen until the last king has passed. 113. **thy hair.** The hair (worn as Banquo doubtless wore it, straight and hanging to the shoulders) is a striking feature and an obvious point of family likeness. Nothing dwelt more fixedly in Macbeth's memory than Banquo's hair; for it had held his gaze at the banquet, matted with blood from the "twenty trenched gashes" (3.4.27). These phantom kings are surely Banquo's descendants—they have *Banquo's hair!* And then, when they have passed by, comes Banquo himself, "blood-bolter'd," as at the feast (3.4.81), "and points at them for his." 117. **crack of doom.** Cf. 1.2.37. 119. **a glass:** a mirror. 121. **balls.** The "ball," "apple," "globe," or "orb" was one of the insignia of sovereignty. *Twofold* refers to England and Scotland. *Treble* refers either to England, Scotland, and Ireland, or, more probably, to the title "King of Great Britain, France, and Ireland," assumed by James I in 1604. Banquo was the mythical ancestor of the Stuarts, of whom James was the first to rule in England. 123. **blood-bolter'd:** having his hair matted with blood. 124–132. As Macbeth is staring at the blood-boltered Banquo, the apparitions vanish, and with a question—"What? Is this *so*?" "Is this the *truth*?"—he turns to the Sisters, only to find that they too have vanished—"Where are they? Gone?" The speech of the First Witch, with the dance, is a manifest interpolation. The idea of cheering up Macbeth by an antic round is worthy of comic opera. The iambic metre is like that of the Hecate speeches and quite different from the trochaic verse which the witches always use except in the interpolated scene (3.5). 126–130. **amazedly:** like a man in a trance. Cf. 2.4.19.—**sprites:** spirits.—**antic:** fantastic.—**round:** dance in a circle. 132. Macbeth has not "welcomed" the Sisters, unless "How now, you secret, black, and midnight hags?" (line 48) can be called a welcome. Nor do they owe him any "duty" (i.e., loyal service). The whole speech is absurdly out of tune.

MACB.   Where are they? Gone? Let this pernicious hour
Stand aye accursed in the calendar!
Come in, without there!

Enter Lennox.

LEN.   What's your Grace's will?   135

MACB.   Saw you the Weird Sisters?

LEN.   No, my lord.

MACB.   Came they not by you?

LEN.   No indeed, my lord.

MACB.   Infected be the air whereon they ride,
And damn'd all those that trust them! I did hear
The galloping of horse. Who was't came by?   140

LEN.   'Tis two or three, my lord, that bring you word
Macduff is fled to England.

MACB.   Fled to England?

LEN.   Ay, my good lord.

MACB.   [*aside*] Time, thou anticipat'st my dread exploits.
The flighty purpose never is o'ertook   145
Unless the deed go with it. From this moment
The very firstlings of my heart shall be
The firstlings of my hand. And even now,
To crown my thoughts with acts, be it thought and done.
The castle of Macduff I will surprise,   150
Seize upon Fife, give to the edge o' th' sword
His wife, his babes, and all unfortunate souls
That trace him in his line. No boasting like a fool.
This deed I'll do before this purpose cool.
But no more sights.—Where are these gentlemen?   155
Come, bring me where they are.   *Exeunt.*

---

135. Lennox has been on guard at the mouth of the cave. 139. **damn'd.** Thus Macbeth, by implication, curses himself, for he trusts the Weird Sisters to the very end (5.8). 140. **horse:** plural or collective— horses or horsemen. 142. **Macduff is fled to England.** Here (as in 1.3.104) the predictions begin to fulfil themselves instantly, and thus their trustworthiness is established in Macbeth's mind (1.3.133). 144. **anticipat'st:** forestallest. 145. **The flighty purpose:** Every purpose is fleeting and will never be fulfilled unless it is accompanied by the act proposed, i.e., unless it is fulfilled as soon as formed. 147. **firstlings:** first-born. The firstlings of his heart are the first purposes that he may form. 150. **surprise:** seize upon suddenly. 152. **unfortunate.** A touch of pity, a remnant of "human kindness" (1.5.13). 153. **trace:** follow. Macduff is the head of his family, and his relatives are therefore said to follow, or come after, him in his line.

SCENE II. [*Fife*. Macduff's *Castle*.]

Enter Macduff's Wife, *her* Son, *and* Ross.

WIFE.   What had he done to make him fly the land?

ROSS.   You must have patience, madam.

WIFE.   He had none.
His flight was madness. When our actions do not,
Our fears do make us traitors.

ROSS.   You know not
Whether it was his wisdom or his fear.   5

WIFE.   Wisdom? To leave his wife, to leave his babes,
His mansion, and his titles, in a place
From whence himself does fly? He loves us not,
He wants the natural touch. For the poor wren,
(The most diminitive of birds) will fight,   10
Her young ones in her nest, against the owl.
All is the fear, and nothing is the love,
As little is the wisdom, where the flight
So runs against all reason.

ROSS.   My dearest coz,
I pray you school yourself. But for your husband,   15
He is noble, wise, judicious, and best knows
The fits o' th' season. I dare not speak much further;
But cruel are the times, when we are traitors
And do not know ourselves; when we hold rumor
From what we fear, yet know not what we fear,   20
But float upon a wild and violent sea
Each way and none. I take my leave of you.

SCENE II.
Between scene 1 and scene 2 the interval is only long enough to enable Macbeth to send the murderers to Macduff's castle. 2. **patience:** self-control. 3, 4. **When...traitors.** Macduff had done nothing treasonable. Yet fear had made him flee to the English court, and this action had made him a traitor in fact. 7. **his titles:** his title deeds, and so—all his hereditary possessions and honors. 9. **the natural touch:** the natural trait which prompts all creatures to fight in defense of their young. 10. **diminitive:** a variant form of *diminutive*. 11. **in her nest:** still being in her nest, and therefore in her charge. 14. **coz:** an affectionate abbreviation of *cousin*. 15. **school yourself:** control yourself.—**for:** as for. 17. **The fits o' th' season:** the fits and starts, the spasmodic and irregular happenings, the strange accidents, that mark this time in Scotland. The metaphor is from a fever fit. 18, 19. **when we...ourselves:** when we are, in the King's eyes, traitors; yet do not know ourselves to be such, are not conscious of having committed treason. 19–22. **when we hold rumor...none:** when every rumor of danger is credited by us because of our fears, and yet we do not really know what there is to be afraid of, since we are not conscious of having committed any offense. Thus we are like a drifting hulk at sea, that is tossed about in every direction by shifting winds but makes no progress in any direction.

	Shall not be long but I'll be here again.	
	Things at the worst will cease, or else climb upward	
	To what they were before.—My pretty cousin,	25
	Blessing upon you.	
WIFE.	Father'd he is, and yet he's fatherless.	
ROSS.	I am so much a fool, should I stay longer,	
	It would be my disgrace and your discomfort.	
	I take my leave at once. *Exit.*	
WIFE.	Sirrah, your father's dead;	30
	And what will you do now? How will you live?	
SON.	As birds do, mother.	
WIFE.	What, with worms and flies?	
SON.	With what I get, I mean; and so do they.	
WIFE.	Poor bird! thou'dst never fear the net nor lime,	
	The pitfall nor the gin.	35
SON.	Why should I, mother? Poor birds they are not set for.	
	My father is not dead, for all your saying.	
WIFE.	Yes, he is dead. How wilt thou do for a father?	
SON.	Nay, how will you do for a husband?	
WIFE.	Why, I can buy me twenty at any market.	40
SON.	Then you'll buy 'em to sell again.	
WIFE.	Thou speak'st with all thy wit; and yet, i' faith,	
	With wit enough for thee.	
SON.	Was my father a traitor, mother?	
WIFE.	Ay, that he was!	45
SON.	What is a traitor?	
WIFE.	Why, one that swears, and lies.	

---

23. **Shall:** it shall. 24. **climb upward:** improve, take a turn for the better. Cf. such proverbs as "The darkest hour is just before the dawn." 29. **It...discomfort:** I should shed tears, which would disgrace me as a man and would distress you to see. The conventional idea that tears are unmanly recurs often in Shakespeare. 30. **Sirrah.** Used in familiar address, sometimes to express anger, contempt, or superiority; often (to boys) as a playful and affectionate term. 34. **lime:** birdlime, a sticky substance daubed on twigs to catch birds. 35. **pitfall:** a kind of trap.—**gin:** short for *engine*; used for any kind of contrivance or device, mental or physical; here, for a snare or the like. 36. **Poor:** Nobody would care to trap a poor little bird like me!—**they:** the net, trap, etc. 42-43. **Thou speak'st...thee:** What you say is childish, for you have but a child's wisdom, even when you use all of it—and yet, for a child, your wit is well enough. *Wit,* as usual, means "intelligence," "sense." 47. **one...lies:** one that takes an oath (of allegiance) and then breaks it.—**be.** An old form of the plural.

SON.	And be all traitors that do so?	
WIFE.	Every one that does so is a traitor and must be hang'd.	
SON.	And must they all be hang'd that swear and lie?	50
WIFE.	Every one.	
SON.	Who must hang them?	
WIFE.	Why, the honest men.	
SON.	Then the liars and swearers are fools; for there are liars and swearers enow to beat the honest men and hang up them.	55
WIFE.	Now God help thee, poor monkey. But how wilt thou do for a father?	
SON.	If he were dead, you'ld weep for him. If you would not, it were a good sign that I should quickly have a new father.	
WIFE.	Poor prattler, how thou talk'st.	60

Enter a Messenger.

MESS.	Bless you, fair dame. I am not to you known, Though in your state of honor I am perfect. I doubt some danger does approach you nearly. If you will take a homely man's advice, Be not found here. Hence with your little ones! To fright you thus methinks I am too savage; To do worse to you were fell cruelty, Which is too nigh your person. Heaven preserve you. I dare abide no longer. *Exit.*	65
WIFE.	Whither should I fly? I have done no harm. But I remember now I am in this earthly world, where to do harm Is often laudable, to do good sometime Accounted dangerous folly. Why then, alas, Do I put up that womanly defense To say I have done no harm?—What are these faces?	70 75

---

55. **enow:** enough (often, but not exclusively, plural). 56. **monkey:** used tenderly, in affection. So *sirrah, wretch, rogue, fool,* and the like. 61. **Bless you:** God bless you. 62. **in your state...perfect:** I am fully informed as to your honorable condition; I know you well, honored lady. 63. **doubt:** fear. 64. **homely:** i.e., of no exalted rank—a plain man, a mere gentleman (not a noble). 66. **To fright you thus:** in frightening you as I do by this warning. 67. **To do worse to you:** i.e., to harm you, as Macbeth intends to do.—**fell:** fierce. 69. **I dare,** etc.: It would be death to myself to be discovered giving you this information. 72. **sometime:** sometimes. 74. **womanly:** womanish. 75. **faces.** As Macbeth sees particularly the *hair* of the apparitions that resemble Banquo (4.1.113), so here the savage *faces* of the murderers so impress themselves on Lady Macduff's imagination that she uses that word for the men themselves. Cf. 5.3.19: "Take thy face hence."

Enter Murderers.

MUR.   Where is your husband?

WIFE.   I hope, in no place so unsanctified
         Where such as thou mayst find him.

MUR.   He's a traitor.

SON.   Thou liest, thou shag-ear'd villain!

MUR.   What, you egg!   [*Stabs him.*]
         Young fry of treachery!

SON.   He has kill'd me, mother.   80
         Run away, I pray you!   [*Dies.*]
                 Exit [*Wife*], *crying* "Murder!" [*and pursued by the Murderers*].

SCENE III. [*England. Before* King Edward's *Palace.*]†

Enter Malcolm *and* Macduff.

MAL.   Let us seek out some desolate shade, and there
         Weep our sad bosoms empty.

MACD.   Let us rather
         Hold fast the mortal sword and, like good men,
         Bestride our downfall'n birthdom. Each new morn
         New widows howl, new orphans cry, new sorrows   5
         Strike heaven on the face, that it resounds
         As if it felt with Scotland and yell'd out
         Like syllable of color.

MAL.   What I believe, I'll wail;

---

79. **shag-ear'd.** The long shaggy hair falling over the ruffian's ears reminds the boy of a dog's ears. The Elizabethan ruffian let his hair grow and prided himself on his unkempt locks.—**egg:** unhatched chick, youngster. 80. **fry:** spawn.
SCENE III.
Between this scene and 3.6, time enough has elapsed to enable Macduff to reach the court of the English king, Edward the Confessor. Macduff has described to Malcolm the oppressive rule of Macbeth and has offered his services, and those of other Scottish nobles, if Malcolm will take command; but Malcolm is unsure, suspecting a trick to get him into Macbeth's power. 3. **mortal:** deadly. 4. **Bestride...birthdom:** fight in defense of our prostrate native land. The figure is from the old hand-to-hand combats, where it was common for a man to bestride a fallen comrade to protect him in a mêlée. —**Each new morn,** etc. Nothing that occurs in the play justifies this description of Macbeth's reign in lines 4–8, but it accords with Holinshed's account. 6. **that:** so that. 8. **Like syllable of color:** words of sorrow that reecho those which all Scotland is uttering.

---

†   The first part of this scene (up to Ross's entrance with his news about Macduff's family) is often
     cut by directors.

What know, believe; and what I can redress,
As I shall find the time to friend, I will.   10
What you have spoke, it may be so perchance.
This tyrant, whose sole name blisters our tongues,
Was once thought honest; you have lov'd him well;
He hath not touch'd you yet. I am young; but something
You may deserve of him through me, and wisdom   15
To offer up a weak, poor, innocent lamb
T' appease an angry god.

MACD.   I am not treacherous.

MAL.   But Macbeth is.
A good and virtuous nature may recoil
In an imperial charge. But I shall crave your pardon.   20
That which you are, my thoughts cannot transpose.
Angels are bright still, though the brightest fell.
Though all things foul would wear the brows of grace,
Yet grace must still look so.

MACD.   I have lost my hopes.

MAL.   Perchance even there where I did find my doubts.   25
Why in that rawness left you wife and child,
Those precious motives, those strong knots of love,
Without leave-taking? I pray you,
Let not my jealousies be your dishonors,
But mine own safeties. You may be rightly just,   30
Whatever I shall think.

---

10. **As...friend:** whenever I find opportunity favorable. *To friend* means "as a friend," and so "friendly."
12. **sole:** mere. 13. **honest:** honorable; good and noble. 14-17. **I am young...god:** Though I am young and inexperienced, I cannot help seeing that you may be trying to entrap me in order to maintain yourself in Macbeth's favor. We learn later that Macbeth has often tried to entice Malcolm back to Scotland (lines 117–119; cf. 3.6.17–20). Perhaps, however, *I am young* means "I am young and helpless, and possibly Macbeth does not worry much about any danger from me."—**deserve:** win, earn.—**through me:** by betraying me into Macbeth's power.—**and wisdom:** and [it is] wisdom. 19-20. **may recoil...charge:** may give way under pressure from a monarch. The figure is either that of retiring before the onslaught (*charge*) of a superior force, or that of a cannon which recoils when the charge (or load) is too great;—**I...pardon:** I must beg your pardon. Malcolm sees indignant grief in Macduff's face. 21. **transpose:** transform. If Macduff is innocent of treachery, Malcolm's suspicions cannot make him guilty. 22. **the brightest:** Lucifer. 23. **would wear:** should strive to wear.—**the brows of grace:** the face or appearance of virtue. 24. **so:** like herself, like virtue. The existence of many hypocrites does not make a good man any the less good, though it may cause him to be mistrusted.—**my hopes:** i.e., my hope of persuading Malcolm to take command in the revolt, and therefore all my hopes for Scotland. 25. **Perchance...doubts:** Perhaps what has made you lose your hopes is the very circumstance that has made me suspicious of you, i.e., your leaving your family in Macbeth's power, as you would hardly have done if you were his enemy. 26. **in that rawness:** in so unprotected a condition. 27. **motives:** incentives to action. 29-30. **Let not...safeties:** Do not regard my suspicions as meant to dishonor you, but rather as proceeding from a due regard for my own safety. All the abstract nouns are plural because the first one is plural.—**rightly just:** perfectly good and honorable.

Macd.	Bleed, bleed, poor country.	
	Great tyranny, lay thou thy basis sure,	
	For goodness dare not check thee. Wear thou thy wrongs;	
	The title is affeer'd. Fare thee well, lord.	
	I would not be the villain that thou think'st	35
	For the whole space that's in the tyrant's grasp	
	And the rich East to boot.	

Macd.   Bleed, bleed, poor country.
Great tyranny, lay thou thy basis sure,
For goodness dare not check thee. Wear thou thy wrongs;
The title is affeer'd. Fare thee well, lord.
I would not be the villain that thou think'st   35
For the whole space that's in the tyrant's grasp
And the rich East to boot.

Mal.   Be not offended.
I speak not as in absolute fear of you.
I think our country sinks beneath the yoke,
It weeps, it bleeds, and each new day a gash   40
Is added to her wounds. I think withal
There would be hands uplifted in my right;
And here from gracious England have I offer
Of goodly thousands. But, for all this,
When I shall tread upon the tyrant's head   45
Or wear it on my sword, yet my poor country
Shall have more vices than it had before,
More suffer and more sundry ways than ever,
By him that shall succeed.

Macd.   What should he be?

Mal.   It is myself I mean; in whom I know   50
All the particulars of vice so grafted
That, when they shall be open'd, black Macbeth
Will seem as pure as snow, and the poor state
Esteem him as a lamb, being compar'd
With my confineless harms.

Macd.   Not in the legions   55
Of horrid hell can come a devil more damn'd
In evils to top Macbeth.

---

32. **tyranny:** usurpation.—**basis:** foundation. 33. **check thee:** rebuke thee; call thee to account.—**Wear thou thy wrongs:** Continue to hold what thou hast wrongly obtained—thy ill-gotten titles and honors. The address is still to "great tyranny" (as personified in Macbeth). 34. **affeer'd:** legally confirmed. Macbeth's title is established beyond dispute, since Malcolm refuses to contest it. 41. **withal:** also, besides. 43. **gracious England:** the good king of England. 44. **But, for all this.** Malcolm's reluctance to trust Macduff has been natural enough. It is not until this point that his curious device for further testing begins. The incident is taken from Holinshed, whom Shakespeare follows rather closely. Its improbability is evident, but in Shakespeare's time it was accepted as historical, and therefore it was available for dramatic treatment. 46. **yet:** after all that. 49. **What should he be?** An amazed and incredulous question: "What worse king could there be than Macbeth?" 51. **particulars:** particular kinds, special varieties.—**grafted:** engrafted, implanted. The figure implies that these faults are so thoroughly incorporated in Malcolm that they have become a part of his very being. 52. **open'd:** developed and brought to view. The figure is from the opening of the bud, and is suggested by the use of *grafted.* 55. **confineless harms:** the boundless injuries that I should do to my people. 57. **top:** surpass.

MAL.   I grant him bloody,
         Luxurious, avaricious, false, deceitful,
         Sudden, malicious, smacking of every sin
         That has a name. But there's no bottom, none,   60
         In my voluptuousness. Your wives, your daughters,
         Your matrons, and your maids could not fill up
         The cistern of my lust; and my desire
         All continent impediments would o'erbear
         That did oppose my will. Better Macbeth   65
         Than such an one to reign.

MACD.   Boundless intemperance
         In nature is a tyranny. It hath been
         Th' untimely emptying of the happy throne
         And fall of many kings. But fear not yet
         To take upon you what is yours. You may   70
         Convey your pleasures in a spacious plenty,
         And yet seem cold—the time you may so hoodwink.
         We have willing dames enough. There cannot be
         That vulture in you to devour so many
         As will to greatness dedicate themselves,   75
         Finding it so inclin'd.

MAL.   With this there grows
         In my most ill-compos'd affection such
         A stanchless avarice that, were I King,
         I should cut off the nobles for their lands,
         Desire his jewels, and this other's house,   80
         And my more-having would be as a sauce
         To make me hunger more, that I should forge
         Quarrels unjust against the good and loyal,
         Destroying them for wealth.

MACD.   This avarice
         Sticks deeper, grows with more pernicious root   85

---

58. **Luxurious:** lascivious. This adjective does not fit Macbeth's character. However, Malcolm is not asserting that it does. He merely admits, for the sake of argument, that Macbeth has every known vice, and then proceeds to describe himself as still worse. 59. **Sudden:** violent. 63. **cistern:** tank, vat. 64. **continent:** restraining. *Continent* is common in the active sense of "holding in," "confining."—**o'erbear:** overpower, sweep away. 65. **will:** desire, lust. 66-67. **Boundless...tyranny:** Boundless incontinence is a tyranny in a man's nature, for it usurps absolute sway over all his other qualities. 71. **Convey:** manage craftily or secretly. 72. **time:** the times, the people. Cf. 1.5.59–60.—**hoodwink:** blindfold, delude. 74-76. **vulture:** ravenous appetite.—**dedicate:** offer up, devote.—**Finding:** if they find. 77. **ill-compos'd affection:** character made up of evil elements. 78. **stanchless:** insatiable.—**that:** so that. 80. **his:** this man's. 81. **more-having:** increase in wealth. 82-83. **forge:** devise falsely.—**Quarrels:** causes of complaint. 85. **Sticks deeper:** is less easily uprooted. If a man is prone to avarice, he is likely to grow worse as he grows older.

	Than summer-seeming lust; and it hath been	
	The sword of our slain kings. Yet do not fear.	
	Scotland hath foisons to fill up your will	
	Of your mere own. All these are portable,	
	With other graces weigh'd.	90

MAL.   But I have none. The king-becoming graces,
        As justice, verity, temp'rance, stableness,
        Bounty, perseverance, mercy, lowliness,
        Devotion, patience, courage, fortitude,
        I have no relish of them, but abound   95
        In the division of each several crime,
        Acting it many ways. Nay, had I pow'r, I should
        Pour the sweet milk of concord into hell,
        Uproar the universal peace, confound
        All unity on earth.

MACD.   O Scotland, Scotland!   100

MAL.   If such a one be fit to govern, speak.
        I am as I have spoken.

MACD.   Fit to govern?
        No, not to live. O nation miserable,
        With an untitled tyrant bloody-scept'red,
        When shalt thou see thy wholesome days again,   105
        Since that the truest issue of thy throne
        By his own interdiction stands accurs'd
        And does blaspheme his breed? Thy royal father
        Was a most sainted king; the queen that bore thee,
        Oft'ner upon her knees than on her feet,   110
        Died every day she liv'd. Fare thee well!
        These evils thou repeat'st upon thyself

---

86. **summer-seeming:** befitting only the summertime of life, the warm and vigorous age, and therefore not lasting so long as avarice. 87. **The sword of our slain kings:** that which has caused their violent death. 88. **foisons:** abundant supplies, stores.—**will:** covetousness. 89-90. **your mere own:** what is absolutely your own property.—**All...weigh'd:** All the vices you have mentioned are endurable, when counterbalanced by other qualities that are virtues. 95-96. **no relish:** no trace, no taste. Cf. line 59.— **abound...crime:** in my actions I am abundantly guilty of every possible form of each sin. 98. **milk.** Cf. 1.5.13, 44; 3.1.67. 99. **Uproar:** change to tumultuous strife. 104. **tyrant:** usurper. Cf. 3.6.22. 107. **interdiction:** the act of putting one 'under the ban' of the Church. Malcolm has virtually pronounced against himself a curse which excludes him from the throne. 108. **does...breed:** slanders his parents by implying that they could naturally produce such a monster. 111. **Died every day she liv'd:** referring to the penances and religious exercises by which she "died to the world." The phrase is a reminiscence of St. Paul's "I die daily" (*1 Corinthians*, xv.31). 112. **repeat'st upon:** recitest against.

Have banish'd me from Scotland. O my breast,
Thy hope ends here!

MAL.   Macduff, this noble passion,
Child of integrity, hath from my soul   115
Wip'd the black scruples, reconcil'd my thoughts
To thy good truth and honor. Devilish Macbeth
By many of these trains hath sought to win me
Into his power; and modest wisdom plucks me
From over-credulous haste; but God above   120
Deal between thee and me! for even now
I put myself to thy direction and
Unspeak mine own detraction, here abjure
The taints and blames I laid upon myself
For strangers to my nature. I am yet   125
Unknown to woman, never was forsworn,
Scarcely have coveted what was mine own,
At no time broke my faith, would not betray
The devil to his fellow, and delight
No less in truth than life. My first false speaking   130
Was this upon myself. What I am truly,
Is thine and my poor country's to command;
Whither indeed, before thy here-approach,
Old Siward with ten thousand warlike men
Already at a point was setting forth.   135
Now we'll together; and the chance of goodness
Be like our warranted quarrel. Why are you silent?

MACD.   Such welcome and unwelcome things at once
'Tis hard to reconcile.

Enter a Doctor.

---

113. **banish'd.** He cannot return to Scotland unless Malcolm becomes king, and Malcolm is not fit to reign. 114. **ends here!** i.e., here and now, as I listen to what you say of yourself.—**passion:** strong emotion. 115. **Child of integrity:** which can proceed only from integrity of character. 116-117. **scruples:** the suspicions that made me hesitate.—**reconcil'd...honor:** brought my opinion of you into accord with your real character as a loyal and honorable man. 118. **trains:** plots, subtle devices (such as he has suspected in Macduff's case).—**win:** entice. 119. **modest wisdom:** wise moderation, i.e., prudent caution.—**plucks me:** pulls me back; restrains me. 121. **Deal...me!** Be judge between us in the matter. This amounts to a solemn oath that what he is about to say is true. 122-123. **to thy direction:** under thy guidance.—**mine own detraction:** the slanderous charges I have brought against myself.—**abjure:** deny solemnly, as upon oath. 124. **taints:** stains, disgraceful accusations. 125. **For...nature:** as being quite foreign to my actual character. 131. **upon:** against. Cf. line 112. 132. **Is...command:** is at your service and at that of my unfortunate country. 134. **Old Siward:** Earl of Northumberland, supporter of King Edward. [A.C.] 135. **at a point:** fully prepared. 136-137. **we'll together:** we'll set out together.— **the chance...quarrel:** may our chance of success be as good as our cause is just! Cf. 1.2.14.

MAL.	Well, more anon. Comes the King forth, I pray you?	140
DOCT.	Ay, sir. There are a crew of wretched souls	
	That stay his cure. Their malady convinces	
	The great assay of art; but at his touch,	
	Such sanctity hath heaven given his hand,	
	They presently amend.	
MAL.	I thank you, doctor. *Exit [Doctor].*	
MACD.	What's the disease he means?	
Mal.	'Tis call'd the evil:	146
	A most miraculous work in this good king,	
	Which often since my here-remain in England	
	I have seen him do. How he solicits heaven	
	Himself best knows; but strangely-visited people,	150
	All swol'n and ulcerous, pitiful to the eye,	
	The mere despair of surgery, he cures,	
	Hanging a golden stamp about their necks,	
	Put on with holy prayers; and 'tis spoken,	
	To the succeeding royalty he leaves	155
	The healing benediction. With this strange virtue,	
	He hath a heavenly gift of prophecy,	
	And sundry blessings hang about his throne	
	That speak him full of grace.	

Enter Ross.

MACD.	See who comes here.	
MAL.	My countryman; but yet I know him not.	160
MACD.	My ever gentle cousin, welcome hither.	

140-159. This passage provides the interval of time needed before the arrival of Ross with the news of the murder of Macduff's wife and children. It also serves as a satisfactory substitute for what might well be expected by the audience, but would encumber the action—the actual appearance of Edward the Confessor on the stage. To Shakespeare's contemporaries the most familiar fact about King Edward was the legend that he was the first English King to cure scrofula, a disease of the lymph nodes, by touching. Incidentally, this episode reminded the audience that James I was descended from a native English ruler as well as (according to tradition) from Banquo. 142-143. **stay:** await.—**convinces...art:** baffles the utmost efforts of medical science. To *convince* is "to conquer utterly" (Latin *convinco*). 145. **presently:** instantly.—**amend:** recover, are made well. 146. **the evil:** scrofula or "the king's evil" (i.e., disease), so called because it was thought to be cured by the royal touch. 148. **my here-remain:** my sojourn here. Cf. l. 133. 149. **solicits heaven:** by prayer prevails upon heaven (to work this miracle). 150. **strangely-visited:** afflicted with hideous disease. Cf. "a visitation of Providence." 152. **The mere despair:** the utter despair; i.e., quite beyond all hope from surgical treatment. 153. **stamp:** a coin which the King gave to the scrofulous patient whom he touched. 155, 156. **the succeeding royalty:** the royal line that shall succeed him.—**virtue:** healing power. 159. **grace:** sanctity, holiness. 160. **My countryman...not.** Malcolm knows that Ross is a Scot from his costume, but he fails to recognize him until he speaks.

MAL.   I know him now. Good God betimes remove
        The means that makes us strangers!

ROSS.   Sir, amen.

MACD.   Stands Scotland where it did?

ROSS.   Alas, poor country,
        Almost afraid to know itself. It cannot   165
        Be call'd our mother, but our grave; where nothing,
        But who knows nothing, is once seen to smile;
        Where sighs and groans, and shrieks that rent the air,
        Are made, not mark'd; where violent sorrow seems
        A modern ecstasy. The dead man's knell   170
        Is there scarce ask'd for who; and good men's lives
        Expire before the flowers in their caps,
        Dying or ere they sicken.

MACD.   O, relation
        Too nice, and yet too true.

MAL.   What's the newest grief?

ROSS.   That of an hour's age doth hiss the speaker;   175
        Each minute teems a new one.

MACD.   How does my wife?

ROSS.   Why, well.

MACD.   And all my children?

ROSS.   Well too.

MACD.   The tyrant has not batter'd at their peace?

ROSS.   No; they were well at peace when I did leave 'em.

MACD.   Be not a niggard of your speech. How goes't?   180

ROSS.   When I came hither to transport the tidings
        Which I have heavily borne, there ran a rumour
        Of many worthy fellows that were out;

---

162. **betimes:** speedily. 163. **The means...strangers!** i.e., Macbeth, who is responsible for Malcolm's absence from Scotland. 165. **to know itself!** to look its own misfortunes in the face! 167-169. **who:** one who.—**rent:** rend.—**not mark'd:** because they are so common. 170. **A modern ecstasy:** an ordinary, commonplace fit of excitement. Cf. 3.2.22. 172. **flowers.** It was an Elizabethan fashion to wear a flower in the cap. 173. **Dying or ere they sicken:** dying before they sicken—i.e., by violence, not a natural death.—**relation:** recital. Cf. 3.4.124. 174. **too nice:** too minutely accurate, because the details are so distressing. 175. **That...speaker:** The report of any dreadful thing that happened but an hour ago causes the teller to be hissed for his stale news, so much has occurred in the interim.—**hour's:** dissyllabic. 176. **teems:** brings forth. 177. **well:** intentionally ambiguous, and often used in breaking bad news gently. It means not only "in good health" but also "well off," i.e., "in heaven." 180. **niggard:** a stingy or miserly person. [A.C.] 182. **heavily:** sadly, sorrowfully. 183. **out:** in the field, under arms.

Which was to my belief witness'd the rather
For that I saw the tyrant's power afoot.   185
Now is the time of help. Your eye in Scotland
Would create soldiers, make our women fight
To doff their dire distresses.

MAL.   Be't their comfort
We are coming thither. Gracious England hath
Lent us good Siward and ten thousand men.   190
An older and a better soldier none
That Christendom gives out.

ROSS.   Would I could answer
This comfort with the like. But I have words
That would be howl'd out in the desert air,
Where hearing should not latch them.

MACD.   What concern they?   195
The general cause? or is it a fee-grief
Due to some single breast?

ROSS.   No mind that's honest
But in it shares some woe, though the main part
Pertains to you alone.

MACD.   If it be mine,
Keep it not from me, quickly let me have it.   200

ROSS.   Let not your ears despise my tongue for ever,
Which shall possess them with the heaviest sound
That ever yet they heard.

MACD.   Humh! I guess at it.

ROSS.   Your castle is surpris'd; your wife and babes
Savagely slaughter'd. To relate the manner,   205
Were, on the quarry of these murder'd deer,
To add the death of you.

MAL.   Merciful heaven!
What, man! Ne'er pull your hat upon your brows.

---

185. **For that:** because.—**power:** forces, troops.—**afoot:** in motion, mobilized. 188. **doff their dire distresses.** Cf. the alliteration in 1.5.66. 189. **England:** the King of England. Cf. 1.2.50. 191–192. **none:** there is none. —**gives out:** publishes, proclaims. There is no one who in all Christendom has the reputation of being an older or a better soldier. 194. **would be:** require to be, should be. Cf. 1.7.34. 195. **latch:** catch. 196, 197. **a fee-grief:** a grief that is one man's possession; a personal sorrow—one that belongs to him alone.—**Due:** belonging.—**honest:** good and honorable. 202. **heaviest:** saddest. Cf. line 182. 204. **surpris'd:** seized, captured. Cf. 4.1.150. 206. **quarry:** slaughtered bodies; literally, the whole amount of game killed in a single hunt. The pun on *deer* and *dear* was so common as not to shock the hearer.

	Give sorrow words. The grief that does not speak	
	Whispers the o'erfraught heart and bids it break.	210

MACD. My children too?

ROSS.   Wife, children, servants, all
That could be found.

MACD.   And I must be from thence?
My wife kill'd too?

ROSS.   I have said.

MAL.   Be comforted.
Let's make us med'cines of our great revenge
To cure this deadly grief.   215

MACD. He has no children. All my pretty ones?
Did you say all? O hell-kite! All?
What, all my pretty chickens and their dam
At one fell swoop?

MAL. Dispute it like a man.

MACD.   I shall do so;   220
But I must also feel it as a man.
I cannot but remember such things were
That were most precious to me. Did heaven look on
And would not take their part? Sinful Macduff,
They were all struck for thee! Naught that I am,   225
Not for their own demerits, but for mine,
Fell slaughter on their souls. Heaven rest them now.

MAL. Be this the whetstone of your sword. Let grief
Convert to anger; blunt not the heart, enrage it.

MACD. O, I could play the woman with mine eyes   230
And braggart with my tongue. But, gentle heavens,
Cut short all intermission. Front to front

---

210. **Whispers…heart:** whispers to the over-burdened heart. *Fraught* means "freighted." 212. **And I must be from thence?** Spoken in bitter self-reproach. "And I must be away from there?" 216. **He has no children:** Two possible meanings, 1) Macbeth has none: if he had, he could not have killed mine. 2) Malcolm has no children, or he would not suggest revenge is a solution to grief. [A.C.] 217. **hell-kite:** hellish bird of prey. 220–221. **Dispute it:** resist it; withstand your grief. 225. **Naught that I am:** wicked man that I am. Macduff blames himself for fleeing from Scotland, thus justifying the language of Lady Macduff in calling his flight "madness" (4.2.3). We are expected, however, to excuse his error of judgment because he could not suspect even Macbeth of such cruelty to the innocent and helpless. 226, 227. **Not for their own demerits.** They were slain because of Macduff's offenses against Macbeth; but that is not quite all that Macduff has in mind. He thinks of their murder as also a judgment sent from God upon his sins in general. 229. **Convert:** change, turn. 230. **play the woman.** See note on 4.2.29. 232. **intermission:** interval of time.—**Front to front:** face to face (literally, forehead to forehead).

Bring thou this fiend of Scotland and myself.
Within my sword's length set him. If he scape,
Heaven forgive him too!

MAL.   This tune goes manly.   235
Come, go we to the King. Our power is ready;
Our lack is nothing but our leave. Macbeth
Is ripe for shaking, and the pow'rs above
Put on their instruments. Receive what cheer you may.
The night is long that never finds the day.   *Exeunt.*

ACT V

SCENE I. [*Dunsinane.* Macbeth's *Castle.*]

Enter a Doctor of Physic *and a* Waiting Gentlewoman.

DOCT.   I have two nights watch'd with you, but can perceive no truth in your
          report. When was it she last walk'd?

GENT.   Since his Majesty went into the field I have seen her rise from her bed,
          throw her nightgown upon her, unlock her closet, take forth paper,
          fold it, write upon't, read it, afterwards seal it, and again return to bed;
          yet all this while in a most fast sleep.   6

---

235. **Heaven...too!** "If I let him escape, I will not only forgive him myself, but I pray God to forgive him also!" Full vengeance, according to an idea that occurs again and again in Elizabethan writers, includes both the death of the offender and his damnation. Complete forgiveness, on the other hand, involves obedience to the biblical precept—"Pray for them which despitefully use you and persecute you" (*Matthew*, v.44). See Macbeth's words to the murderers in 3.1.88–91. 236. **power:** forces (as in line 185). 237. **Our...leave:** Nothing remains to do except to take our leave of King Edward and receive his permission to depart. 238. **ripe for shaking.** The figure is from ripe fruit which is ready to fall when the tree is shaken. 239. **Put on their instruments:** are urging us, their agents, to action. The war upon which they are entering is, then, a "holy war."—**cheer:** comfort.—**may:** can.

ACT V. SCENE I.
After the long scene that closes the fourth Act, we feel that much time has elapsed since we have seen Lady Macbeth, and are ready to believe that the nervous strain under which several speeches of hers (especially 3.2. 4–7) have shown that she was gradually giving way, may have broken her down at last. Thus we are prepared for the infinite horror and pathos of the scene which follows. This scene is in prose for an obvious reason. The disjointed, incoherent utterances of Lady Macbeth call for it. Metre would deprive them, by its very regularity, of their incoherence and fragmentary character. In the present case, there is the further reason that the simplicity of style and matter which the subject and the situation call for, is best expressed in prose. The speeches of the Doctor and the Waiting Gentlewoman are to sound as much like real conversation as possible. 3. **went into the field.** Macbeth had taken the field against his rebellious subjects (the "many worthy fellows that were out") before Ross went to England (see 4.3.185). 4. **nightgown:** dressing gown (as in 2.2.70). 6. **this while:** this time.

DOCT. A great perturbation in nature, to receive at once the benefit of sleep and do the effects of watching! In this slumb'ry agitation, besides her walking and other actual performances, what (at any time) have you heard her say?   10

GENT. That, sir, which I will not report after her.

DOCT. You may to me, and 'tis most meet you should.

GENT. Neither to you nor any one, having no witness to confirm my speech.

Enter Lady [Macbeth], *with a taper.*†

Lo you, here she comes! This is her very guise, and, upon my life, fast asleep! Observe her; stand close.   15

DOCT. How came she by that light?

GENT. Why, it stood by her. She has light by her continually. 'Tis her command.

DOCT. You see her eyes are open.

GENT. Ay; but their sense is shut.   20

DOCT. What is it she does now? Look how she rubs her hands.

GENT. It is an accustom'd action with her, to seem thus washing her hands. I have known her continue in this a quarter of an hour.

LADY. Yet here's a spot.‡

DOCT. Hark, she speaks! I will set down what comes from her, to satisfy my remembrance the more strongly.   26

7-10. The professional elevation of the Doctor's language is noteworthy. Physicians were, and still are, expected to speak of their patients' ailments in a dignified and rather technical fashion.—**effects of watching:** the acts proper to a waking condition.—**slumb'ry agitation:** disturbed action in sleep.—**actual performances:** performances in the way of acts. 12. **meet:** fitting, proper. 14. **her very guise:** the exact way in which I have described her appearance. 15. **close:** out of sight, in concealment. They draw back instinctively, for Lady Macbeth's eyes are open, though they know that she cannot see them. Thus the centre of the stage is left to her. 20. **their sense:** their faculty of sight. 24. **Yet:** after all this washing. 25. **satisfy:** reinforce, confirm.

---

†   Polanski had Annis perform the sleepwalking scene in the nude, but rather than conferring extraneous sexuality, her lack of clothing only makes her more fragile and vulnerable. In *Men of Respect* Ruthie wanders the garden with a flashlight and washes her hands in the birdbath. [A.C.]

‡   In *Scotland, PA*, the Lady Macbeth character imagines her hand is burned rather than bloodied, since she was originally burned when Duncan fell into the fryer. She first buys various ointments and then takes to wearing gloves to cover the disfigurement that only she can see. [A.C.]

LADY.	Out, damned spot! out, I say! One; two. Why then 'tis time to do't. Hell is murky. Fie, my lord, fie! a soldier, and afeard? What need we fear who knows it, when none can call our pow'r to accompt? Yet who would have thought the old man to have had so much blood in him?
DOCT.	Do you mark that? 31
LADY.	The Thane of Fife had a wife. Where is she now? What, will these hands ne'er be clean? No more o' that, my lord, no more o' that! You mar all with this starting.
DOCT.	Go to, go to! You have known what you should not. 35
GENT.	She has spoke what she should not, I am sure of that. Heaven knows what she has known.
LADY.	Here's the smell of the blood still. All the perfumes of Arabia will not sweeten this little hand. Oh, oh, oh!
DOCT.	What a sigh is there! The heart is sorely charg'd. 40
GENT.	I would not have such a heart in my bosom for the dignity of the whole body.
DOCT.	Well, well, well.
GENT.	Pray God it be, sir.
DOCT.	This disease is beyond my practice. Yet I have known those which have walk'd in their sleep who have died holily in their beds. 46
LADY.	Wash your hands, put on your nightgown, look not so pale! I tell you yet again, Banquo's buried. He can not come out on's grave.
DOCT.	Even so?
LADY.	To bed, to bed! There's knocking at the gate. Come, come, come, come, give me your hand! What's done cannot be undone. To bed, to bed, to bed! *Exit.* 52

---

27. **One; two.** The murder of Duncan, then, was committed soon after two o'clock in the morning. 28–30. **Fie...in him?** This repeats what she said to her husband in the interval between 2.2 and 2.3, after they had retired to their chamber to "wash this filthy witness from their hands." 29. **accompt:** account. 32. **Thane of Fife:** Macduff. [A.C.] 33-34. **No more o' that...starting.** A reminiscence of the banquet scene (3.4.63): "O, these flaws and starts." 35. **Go to!** Here an exclamation of reproof. It means literally "Go away!" and, like our colloquial *Go way!* (which is an old idiom) may be used in expostulation, reproof, impatience, or incredulity. Sometimes it merely closes or shuts off discussion like "Very well!" or "Enough said!" 40. **charg'd:** burdened. 44. The Gentlewoman catches up the Doctor's vaguely pensive "well" and gives it a definite meaning. 45. **beyond my practice:** beyond my ability to cure; not, outside of my experience. It is one of those cases in which "the patient must minister to himself" (5.3.45–46). 47. **Wash your hands.** Here, in her dream, she confuses the two murders, Duncan's and Banquo's. 48. **yet again:** as she had told him in the interval between the scenes after the close of 3.4. In this interval he had of course talked of Banquo's murder and of the ghost.—**on's:** of his. 51. **What's...undone.** An echo of her words in 3.2.12: "What's done is done." Cf. 1.7.1–2.

DOCT.	Will she go now to bed?
GENT.	Directly.

DOCT.   Foul whisp'rings are abroad. Unnatural deeds   55
   Do breed unnatural troubles. Infected minds
   To their deaf pillows will discharge their secrets.
   More needs she the divine than the physician.
   God, God forgive us all. Look after her;
   Remove from her the means of all annoyance,   60
   And still keep eyes upon her. So good night.
   My mind she has mated, and amaz'd my sight.
   I think, but dare not speak.

GENT.   Good night, good doctor. *Exeunt.*

SCENE II. [*The country near Dunsinane.*]

Drum and Colors. Enter Menteith, Caithness, Angus, Lennox, Soldiers.

MENT.   The English pow'r is near, led on by Malcolm,
   His uncle Siward, and the good Macduff.
   Revenges burn in them; for their dear causes
   Would to the bleeding and the grim alarm
   Excite the mortified man.

ANG.   Near Birnam Wood   5
   Shall we well meet them; that way are they coming.

CAITH.   Who knows if Donalbain be with his brother?

LEN.   For certain, sir, he is not. I have a file
   Of all the gentry. There is Siward's son

---

55. **Foul whisp'rings.** The Doctor has heard rumours of Macbeth's guilt. Cf. 3.1.1–3, 30–33.
56. **Infected:** diseased because of guilt. Cf. 5.3.40. 57. **discharge:** unload, reveal. Cf. line 60. 60.
annoyance: injury. He fears suicide, and justly, as the sequel shows (5.8.70–71). 61. **still:** always. 62.
mated: paralyzed (so that I know not what to think). To *mate* is "to take the life out of."—**amaz'd:**
reduced to utter confusion (so that I can hardly believe what I have seen).

SCENE II.
Many of the Scottish nobles had revolted before Ross went to England, and Macbeth had taken the
field against them (4.3.181–185); but he has been forced to retire to the strong castle of Dunsinane. The
malcontents are now marching to join the army which they hear Malcolm is leading from England.
1. pow'r: forces, army. **2. uncle.** In Holinshed, Malcolm's mother is Earl Siward's daughter. **3. dear
causes:** heartfelt causes, appealing to their deepest and strongest emotions. *Dear* is used of anything
that comes near to one's heart or interests: the nearness may be pleasant or unpleasant, friendly or
hostile. **4, 5. Would...man:** would rouse to action even a paralytic and make him join the rest in the
fierce and bloody onset.—**bleeding:** bloody (adj. with *alarm*).—**alarm:** call to arms—hence, rally,
on-set, attack.—**mortified:** paralyzed (literally, deadened). **6. well:** probably; very likely. **8. file:** list
(as in 3.1.94).

	And many unrough youths that even now	10
	Protest their first of manhood.	
MENT.	What does the tyrant?	
CAITH.	Great Dunsinane he strongly fortifies.	
	Some say he's mad; others, that lesser hate him,	
	Do call it valiant fury; but for certain	
	He cannot buckle his distemper'd cause	15
	Within the belt of rule.	

ANG.   Now does he feel
His secret murders sticking on his hands.
Now minutely revolts upbraid his faith-breach.
Those he commands move only in command,
Nothing in love. Now does he feel his title   20
Hang loose about him, like a giant's robe
Upon a dwarfish thief.

MENT.   Who then shall blame
His pester'd senses to recoil and start,
When all that is within him does condemn
Itself for being there?

CAITH.   Well, march we on   25
To give obedience where 'tis truly ow'd.
Meet we the med'cine of the sickly weal;
And with him pour we in our country's purge
Each drop of us.

LEN.   Or so much as it needs
To dew the sovereign flower and drown the weeds.   30
Make we our march towards Birnam.   *Exeunt, marching*

10-11. **unrough:** smooth-faced, beardless.—**Protest...manhood:** declare (by going to war) that they are now first acting a man's part.—**tyrant:** usurper. 14. **valiant fury:** the frenzy of desperate valor. 15-16. **He cannot...rule:** The cause for which he fights is so bad that he cannot restrain himself within the bounds of self-control in supporting it. *Rule* means "self-government."—**distemper'd:** literally, diseased. The figure is of a dropsical person, swollen beyond the limits of a normal girdle. The purpose of lines 11–24 is to prepare us for the almost maniacal excitement which Macbeth is to show in the next scene and which is quite different from his demeanour heretofore. 17. **sticking on his hands.** A graphic figure, suggesting the viscous quality of coagulated blood, and reminding us of Lady Macbeth's efforts to wash it from her hands. 18. **minutely:** every minute.—**upbraid:** for every time a noble revolts, it reminds him of his own breach of faith— "th' ingredience of our poison'd chalice" again (1.7.11). 19. **in:** because of. 20. **Nothing:** not at all. 23. **pester'd senses:** tormented mind.—**to recoil and start:** for giving way and becoming distracted. 24, 25. **When all...there:** for, when he looks into his mind, he sees nothing but consciousness of guilt. 27. **the med'cine of the sickly weal:** the physician who is to restore the commonweal to a healthy condition, i.e., Malcolm, whose army these nobles intend to join. Macbeth uses the same metaphor in 5.3.50–56, dwelling on it with all the vivid detail of his poetical imagination. 28. **our country's purge:** the physic (cleansing draught) that is to purge our country of its present evils. "Let us shed every drop of our blood to help Malcolm to deliver Scotland from Macbeth and his tyranny."

SCENE III. [*Dunsinane. A room in the Castle.*]

Enter *Macbeth, Doctor,* and *Attendants.*

MACB. Bring me no more reports. Let them fly all!
Till Birnam Wood remove to Dunsinane,
I cannot taint with fear. What's the boy Malcolm?
Was he not born of woman? The spirits that know
All mortal consequences have pronounc'd me thus: 5
"Fear not, Macbeth. No man that's born of woman
Shall e'er have power upon thee." Then fly, false thanes,
And mingle with the English epicures.
The mind I sway by and the heart I bear
Shall never sag with doubt nor shake with fear.   10

Enter Servant.

The devil damn thee black, thou cream-fac'd loon!
Where got'st thou that goose look?

SERV. There is ten thousand—

MACB.   Geese, villain?

SERV.   Soldiers, sir.

MACB. Go prick thy face and over-red thy fear,
Thou lily-liver'd boy. What soldiers, patch?   15
Death of thy soul! Those linen cheeks of thine
Are counsellors to fear. What soldiers, whey-face?

SERV. The English force, so please you.

MACB. Take thy face hence.   [*Exit Servant.*]

SCENE III.
This scene doubtless takes place on the day after scene 1, for in it Macbeth receives the Doctor's report of Lady Macbeth's condition. Scenes 2 and 3, then, belong to the same day. Macbeth has had news of the revolt of the Scottish nobles and of their intention to join the English army of invasion. Scene 2 has prepared us for his wild demeanor, which some call "valiant fury." 3. **taint:** become tainted. 5. **mortal consequences:** not, results; but simply, future events in human life. Cf. 1.7.3: "trammel up the consequence." 8. **epicures.** The English were regarded by the Scots as living in luxurious plenty. 9. **The mind I sway by:** the mind by which I move (literally, swing), i.e., the mind which governs my actions. 10. **sag,** etc.: in prose order—The mind I sway by shall never sag (give way, sink) with doubt, and the heart I bear shall never shake with fear. **The devil,** etc. Here the ungoverned demeanor of Macbeth, for which scene 2 has prepared us, breaks out into a frenzy which may well have been called "madness."—**loon:** fool. 15. **lily-liver'd:** white-livered, cowardly. Fear was supposed to be caused by lack of red blood in the liver.—**patch:** fool. 16. **Death of thy soul!** A curse: Death upon thy soul. 17. **Are counsellors to fear:** prompt others to fear. Macbeth does not mean that the servant's white cheeks alarm *him,* but that they tend to infect his other followers with fear.—**whey-face:** pale-faced fellow. 19. **Take thy face hence.** A fine example of focused impression. All that Macbeth sees of the servant is his white, panic-stricken face. So in the vision of the kings, what caught and held Macbeth's eye was the *hair,* so like Banquo's (4.1.113–114). Cf. also Lady Macduff's words when the murderers burst in (4.2.75): "What are these faces?"

Seyton!—I am sick at heart,
When I behold—Seyton, I say!—This push   20
Will cheer me ever, or disseat me now.
I have liv'd long enough. My way of life
Is fall'n into the sere, the yellow leaf;
And that which should accompany old age,
As honor, love, obedience, troops of friends,   25
I must not look to have; but, in their stead,
Curses not loud but deep, mouth-honor, breath,
Which the poor heart would fain deny, and dare not.
Seyton!

Enter Seyton.

SEY.   What's your gracious pleasure?

MACB.   What news more?   30

SEY.   All is confirm'd, my lord, which was reported.

MACB.   I'll fight, till from my bones my flesh be hack'd.
Give me my armor.

SEY.   'Tis not needed yet.

MACB.   I'll put it on.
Send out moe horses, skirr the country round;   35
Hang those that talk of fear. Give me mine armor.
How does your patient, doctor?

DOCT.   Not so sick, my lord,
As she is troubled with thick-coming fancies
That keep her from her rest.

MACB.   Cure her of that!
Canst thou not minister to a mind diseas'd,   40

—**sick at heart.** His frenzy gives place, in an instant, to profound dejection. 20. **This push:** this final effort. 21. **Will cheer...now:** will either give me peace and happiness for ever or dethrone me instantly and once for all. Cf. "To be thus is nothing, But to be safely thus" (3.1.47–48), and "Whom we, to gain our peace, have sent to peace" (3.2.20); 22-29. **My way of life,** etc.: My life in its course has declined into the autumn (the season of dry and yellow leaves); and when old age comes, I must not look to have, etc.—**honor...friends.** Macbeth contrasts the desolate old age to which he looks forward with the serene old age of the gracious Duncan, just as he has already contrasted with his own life of "restless ecstasy" the peaceful sleep that Duncan enjoys in the grave (3.2.16–26).—**mouth-honor.** The antithesis is between *mouth* and *heart.* All that Macbeth can expect is homage in words, which the heart of the liegeman does not prompt, but would refuse if it dared. Cf. 3.6.36: "Do faithful homage and receive free honors." 32. **I'll fight.** Macbeth's personal courage, the quality which is first emphasized in the tragedy (1.2), remains with him to the last. 35. **moe:** more (not a clipped form of that word, but a different formation from the same root).—**skirr:** ride rapidly, scour (cf. *scurry*). 37. **Not so sick:** not so much afflicted with any bodily ailment. 39. **Cure her of that!** That is the very thing of which I wish you to cure her. I called you to the castle for that very purpose.

Pluck from the memory a rooted sorrow,
Raze out the written troubles of the brain,
And with some sweet oblivious antidote
Cleanse the stuff'd bosom of that perilous stuff
Which weighs upon the heart?

DOCT.   Therein the patient   45
Must minister to himself.

MACB.   Throw physic to the dogs, I'll none of it!—
Come, put mine armor on. Give me my staff.—
Seyton, send out.—Doctor, the thanes fly from me.—
Come, sir, dispatch.—If thou couldst, doctor, cast   50
The water of my land, find her disease,
And purge it to a sound and pristine health,
I would applaud thee to the very echo,
That should applaud again.—Pull't off, I say.—
What rhubarb, senna, or what purgative drug,   55
Would scour these English hence? Hear'st thou of them?

DOCT.   Ay, my good lord. Your royal preparation
Makes us hear something.

MACB.   Bring it after me.
I will not be afraid of death and bane
Till Birnam Forest come to Dunsinane. [*Exeunt all but the Doctor.*] 60

DOCT.   Were I from Dunsinane away and clear,
Profit again should hardly draw me here.   *Exit.*

---

42. **Raze out:** erase, as from a waxed tablet. 43. **oblivious:** causing oblivion or utter forgetfulness. 44. **the stuff'd bosom:** "the o'erfraught heart" (4.3.210). 49. **Doctor, the thanes fly from me.** A masterly touch. All physicians, by their very profession, invite confidences. That the King should turn to him in this familiar way suggests also the need he feels of a faithful friend. 50–51. **Come, sir, dispatch:** make haste—addressed to the squire who is putting on Macbeth's armor.—**cast...land:** make a diagnosis of the disease from which Scotland is suffering. A medical figure from examination of a patient's urine. 52. **pristine:** such as she enjoyed in former times. 54. **Pull't off, I say:** i.e., some part of his armor, which Macbeth, in his restlessness, has got on wrong. 56. **scour:** purge, clear away (as by a violent purgative medicine). 58. **Bring it after me!** i.e., the piece of armor which has just been taken off. 59-62. **I will not...here.** The two rhyme-tags are significant of the action. Each marks an exit. Macbeth goes off the stage, uttering the first. This leaves the Doctor alone, and he shakes his head, looks grave, and follows, wishing himself well out of the dangerous situation in which he can do no good.—**bane:** destruction.

SCENE IV. [*Country near Birnam Wood.*]

Drum and Colors. Enter Malcolm, Siward, Macduff, Siward's Son, Menteith, Caithness, Angus, [Lennox, Ross,] *and* Soldiers, *marching.*

MAL.	Cousins, I hope the days are near at hand That chambers will be safe.
MENT.	We doubt it nothing.
SIW.	What wood is this before us?
MENT.	The Wood of Birnam.
MAL.	Let every soldier hew him down a bough And bear't before him. Thereby shall we shadow 5 The numbers of our host and make discovery Err in report of us.
SOLDIERS.	It shall be done.
SIW.	We learn no other but the confident tyrant Keeps still in Dunsinane and will endure Our setting down before't.
MAL.	'Tis his main hope; 10 For where there is advantage to be given, Both more and less have given him the revolt; And none serve with him but constrained things, Whose hearts are absent too.
MACD.	Let our just censures Attend the true event, and put we on 15 Industrious soldiership.

SCENE IV.

The Scottish nobles who had taken the field against Macbeth have now joined forces with Malcolm at Birnam Wood according to their plan in scene 2. 2. **nothing:** not at all. 4. **Let every soldier,** etc. This stratagem is a very old piece of popular fiction and is widespread in folk-tales. 6. **discovery:** Macbeth's scouts. 8. **no other:** nothing else. 10. **setting down:** encampment for laying siege. 11. **advantage... given.** To *give advantage* is "to offer or afford an opportunity." The whole clause means, "wherever the circumstances are such that an opportunity can be afforded them" or "can offer itself." 12. **more and less:** high and low; nobles and commoners. 13. **things:** used contemptuously for persons who, being constrained, have no will of their own and are therefore mere instruments rather than men. 14–16. **hearts...too:** as well as the *bodies* of those who have actually revolted. Cf. 4.3.235.—**Let...soldiership:** Let our opinions, in order that they may be accurate, wait for the outcome, which is sure to disclose the truth; and meantime let us use all our skill and energy in the campaign. Macduff, though confident enough of the issue, is older and less sanguine than Malcolm. He knows that Macbeth has not lost all his resources of defence. Siward (lines 16–21) repeats the thought of Macduff in different language.— **put we on:** a metaphor from clothing (with armor). Cf. 1.3.108, 145; 5.2.21.—**industrious:** energetic.

SIW.   The time approaches
        That will with due decision make us know
        What we shall say we have, and what we owe.
        Thoughts speculative their unsure hopes relate,
        But certain issue strokes must arbitrate;   20
        Towards which advance the war.   *Exeunt, marching.*

SCENE V. [*Dunsinane. Within the Castle.*]

Enter *Macbeth, Seyton,* and *Soldiers,* with *Drum* and *Colors.*

MACB.   Hang out our banners on the outward walls.
        The cry is still, 'They come!' Our castle's strength
        Will laugh a siege to scorn. Here let them lie
        Till famine and the ague eat them up.
        Were they not forc'd with those that should be ours,   5
        We might have met them dareful, beard to beard,
        And beat them backward home.
                                    A cry within of women.
                            What is that noise?

SEY.   It is the cry of women, my good lord.   [*Exit.*]

MACB.   I have almost forgot the taste of fears.
        The time has been, my senses would have cool'd   10
        To hear a night-shriek, and my fell of hair
        Would at a dismal treatise rouse and stir
        As life were in't. I have supp'd full with horrors.
        Direness, familiar to my slaughterous thoughts,
        Cannot once start me.

                        [*Enter* Seyton.]
                    Wherefore was that cry?   15

---

18. **What...owe.** *Say* and *owe* are the emphatic words: "What we shall merely *claim* as our own and what we shall actually *possess.*" At present there is a wide difference between what Malcolm and his party *say* belongs to them and what they really *have* in their possession. The battle will decide whether this distinction is to be permanent. 21. **Towards which:** towards which strokes; towards the fight.
SCENE V.
1. **the outward walls.** Dunsinane is a large castle with various walls and fortifications, which must be taken one after another. 2. **still:** always. 3. **lie:** lie encamped. 4. **famine and the ague.** These were inseparable from a long siege in old times. *Ague* is used for "pestilence" in general. It would have been almost impossible for the invaders to take Dunsinane if the garrison had remained faithful to Macbeth. 5. **forc'd:** reinforced. 6. **met them:** i.e., in the field.—**dareful:** boldly. 8. 9. **forgot the taste of fears:** forgotten what dreadful things are like. *Fears* means "objects or causes of fear." Cf. 1.3.137. 10. **cool'd:** felt the chill of terror. 11. **my fell of hair:** the hair upon my skin. Cf. *Job,* iv.13–15: "In thoughts from the visions of the night, when deep sleep falleth on men, fear came upon me, and trembling, which made all my bones to shake. Then a spirit passed before my face: the hair of my flesh stood up." 12. **treatise:** story. Cf. 3.4.63–66. 13. **As:** as if. 14. **Direness:** horror. 15. **start:** startle. Cf. 3.4.63; 5.2.23.

SEY.	The Queen, my lord, is dead.
MACB.	She should have died hereafter;

MACB. She should have died hereafter;
There would have been a time for such a word.
Tomorrow, and tomorrow, and tomorrow
Creeps in this petty pace from day to day   20
To the last syllable of recorded time;
And all our yesterdays have lighted fools
The way to dusty death. Out, out, brief candle!
Life's but a walking shadow, a poor player,
That struts and frets his hour upon the stage   25
And then is heard no more. It is a tale
Told by an idiot, full of sound and fury,
Signifying nothing.

Enter a Messenger.

Thou com'st to use thy tongue. Thy story quickly.

MESS. Gracious my lord,   30
I should report that which I say I saw,
But know not how to do't.

MACB.   Well, say, sir.

MESS. As I did stand my watch upon the hill,
I look'd toward Birnam, and anon methought
The wood began to move.

MACB.   Liar and slave!   35

MESS. Let me endure your wrath if't be not so.
Within this three mile may you see it coming;
I say, a moving grove.

MACB.   If thou speak'st false,
Upon the next tree shalt thou hang alive,

17–18. **should:** means (as very often) "inevitably or certainly would." *Word* is "message." Macbeth receives the news of his wife's death with apathy, and does not even ask the manner or the cause. "Ah, well! she would certainly have died *sometime*! some day this message must have come." 21. **recorded time:** i.e., time, as opposed to eternity (in which there are no yesterdays and no tomorrows). *Syllable* is used because Macbeth is thinking of events as recorded as they happen, one after another, until the last syllable of human history has been registered and time is merged in eternity. 22. **fools:** used of men in general—us poor, weak, ignorant mortals. 23. **brief:** short-lived. 24. **a poor player.** The emphatic word is not *poor,* but *player.* The adjective is not meant to confine the comparison to *bad* actors but is of general application. It is the pathos of the actor's lot that his art perishes with him: he leaves nothing behind but a fading memory. *Poor,* then, expresses pity: "Life is like an actor, who, poor fellow, struts and frets his hour," etc.—**struts and frets** shows Macbeth's contempt, not for the actor, but for human life. The player does not act real life, he only imitates it; but after all, life itself is as poor a thing, as much of a mockery of reality, as the player's art is a mockery of life; and both life and the actor's art are pitifully transitory things. 30. **Gracious my lord.** Cf. 3.2.27. 35. **Liar and slave!** Macbeth's frenzy, alternating with his apathy, shows itself in passionate abuse, as in 5.3.

Till famine cling thee. If thy speech be sooth,   40
I care not if thou dost for me as much.
I pull in resolution, and begin
To doubt th' equivocation of the fiend,
That lies like truth. 'Fear not, till Birnam wood
Do come to Dunsinane!' and now a wood   45
Comes toward Dunsinane. Arm, arm, and out!
If this which he avouches does appear,
There is nor flying hence nor tarrying here.
I gin to be aweary of the sun,
And wish th' estate o' th' world were now undone.   50
Ring the alarm bell! Blow wind, come wrack,
At least we'll die with harness on our back!   *Exeunt.*

SCENE VI. [*Dunsinane. Before the Castle.*]

Drum and Colors. Enter Malcolm, Siward, Macduff, *and their* Army, *with boughs.*

MAL.   Now near enough. Your leavy screens throw down
            And show like those you are. You, worthy uncle,
            Shall with my cousin, your right noble son,
            Lead our first battle. Worthy Macduff and we
            Shall take upon's what else remains to do,   5
            According to our order.

SIW.   Fare you well.
            Do we but find the tyrant's power tonight,
            Let us be beaten if we cannot fight.

MACD.   Make all our trumpets speak, give them all breath,
            Those clamorous harbingers of blood and death.   10
                            Exeunt. Alarms continued.

---

40. **cling thee:** waste thee away till thy skin sticks to thy bones.—**sooth:** truth. 42. **pull in:** rein in, check. "I can no longer give free rein to confidence and determination." 43. **To doubt...fiend:** to suspect that Satan has been cheating me by his regular device of ambiguous prophecies. 47. **avouches:** protests is true, vouches for, asserts. 49. **gin:** begin. 50. **th' estate o' th' world:** the orderly universe.—**undone:** returned to chaos. 51. **alarum bell.** Cf. 2.3.70.—**wrack:** ruin, destruction. 52. **harness:** armor.
SCENE VI.
This short scene is rather formal in style, as befits a scene intended merely to convey information and advance the plot, not to depict character or express passion. 1. **leavy:** leafy. 2. **show:** appear.—**worthy:** noble.—**uncle:** Siward. Cf. 5.2.2. 4. **battle:** battalion, division, troop.—**we.** Malcolm makes significant use of the royal *we*. 5. **upon's:** upon us.—**what:** whatever. 6. **our order:** the arrangements we have already made. 7. **Do we:** if we do.—**power:** forces.

SCENE VII. [*Another part of the field.*]

Enter Macbeth.

MACB.   They have tied me to a stake. I cannot fly,
            But bear-like I must fight the course. What's he
            That was not born of woman? Such a one
            Am I to fear, or none.

Enter Young Siward.

Y. SIW.   What is thy name?

MACB.   Thou'lt be afraid to hear it.   5

Y. SIW.   No; though thou call'st thyself a hotter name
            Than any is in hell.

MACB.   My name's Macbeth.

Y. SIW.   The devil himself could not pronounce a title
            More hateful to mine ear.

MACB.   No, nor more fearful.

Y. SIW.   Thou liest, abhorred tyrant! With my sword   10
            I'll prove the lie thou speak'st.

Fight, and Young Siward slain.

MACB.   Thou wast born of woman.
            But swords I smile at, weapons laugh to scorn,
            Brandish'd by man that's of a woman born.   *Exit.*

Alarums. Enter Macduff.

MACD.   That way the noise is. Tyrant, show thy face!
            If thou beest slain and with no stroke of mine,   15
            My wife and children's ghosts will haunt me still.
            I cannot strike at wretched kerns, whose arms
            Are hir'd to bear their staves. Either thou, Macbeth,
            Or else my sword with an unbattered edge
            I sheathe again undeeded. There thou shouldst be.   20

SCENE VII.
The encounter with young Siward is necessary to the suspense. Its result encourages Macbeth to trust "the fiend" still, though so often deceived by "equivocation." 1. **tied me to a stake.** A figure from bear-baiting, in which the bear was tied to a post and attacked by dogs. Macbeth's castle is surrounded, so that he cannot escape. He has made a sally (5.5.46), but has failed to break through the besiegers and has retired to his defenses. 2. **the course.** A course was one "running" at the bear by the dogs, a "bout." 16. **still:** forever. The word does not imply (as it would in modern English) that they had already haunted him. 17. **kerns.** See 1.2.13. Here used in the general sense of "mercenary soldiers." 18. **staves:** spears. 20. **undeeded:** not honored by any feat of arms.—**shouldst be:** ought to be, to judge by the din.

	By this great clatter one of greatest note	
	Seems bruited. Let me find him, Fortune,	
	And more I beg not.	*Exit. Alarms.*

Enter Malcolm *and* Siward.

SIW.   This way, my lord. The castle's gently rend'red:
         The tyrant's people on both sides do fight;   25
         The noble thanes do bravely in the war;
         The day almost itself professes yours,
         And little is to do.

MAL.   We have met with foes
         That strike beside us.

SIW.   Enter, sir, the castle.   *Exeunt. Alarm.*

SCENE VIII. *Another part of the field.*

Enter Macbeth.

MACB.   Why should I play the Roman fool and die
         On mine own sword? Whiles I see lives, the gashes
         Do better upon them.

Enter Macduff.

MACD.   Turn, hellhound, turn!

MACB.   Of all men else I have avoided thee.
         But get thee back! My soul is too much charg'd   5
         With blood of thine already.

MACD.   I have no words;
         My voice is in my sword, thou bloodier villain
         Than terms can give thee out!   *Fight. Alarm.*

MACB.   Thou losest labor.
         As easy mayst thou the intrenchant air
         With thy keen sword impress as make me bleed.   10

---

22. **bruited:** reported, proclaimed. 24. **gently rend'red:** surrendered without active defense. 26. **bravely:** finely, splendidly. 27. **professes:** declares itself. 29. **strike beside us:** let their blows fall by our sides without trying to hit us—a natural hyperbole to express the half-heartedness of Macbeth's followers.
SCENE VIII.
1. **the Roman fool:** like Brutus in *Julius Cæsar* or Cato Uticensis or Mark Antony (who is mentioned by Macbeth in 3.1.56). 2. **Whiles...lives:** so long as I see any of the enemy alive. 4. **avoided thee.** Macbeth has avoided Macduff because of the warning of the apparition in 4.1.71: "Beware Macduff." But there is another reason, given in what follows: he feels sure that Macduff will fall if they fight. There is still a drop of the milk of human kindness in his veins. 5. **charg'd:** loaded, burdened. Cf. 5.1.40. 8. **Than...out:** than words can declare thee. Cf. 4.3.192. 9. **mayst:** canst.—**intrenchant:** that cannot be gashed or wounded. See 3.4.27. 10. **impress:** make an impression on.

Let fall thy blade on vulnerable crests.
I bear a charmed life, which must not yield
To one of woman born.

MACD.   Despair thy charm!
And let the angel whom thou still hast serv'd
Tell thee, Macduff was from his mother's womb   15
Untimely ripp'd.

MACB.   Accursed be that tongue that tells me so,
For it hath cow'd my better part of man!
And be these juggling fiends no more believ'd,
That palter with us in a double sense,   20
That keep the word of promise to our ear
And break it to our hope! I'll not fight with thee!

MACD.   Then yield thee, coward,
And live to be the show and gaze o' th' time!
We'll have thee, as our rarer monsters are,   25
Painted upon a pole, and underwrit
"Here may you see the tyrant."

MACB.   I will not yield,
To kiss the ground before young Malcolm's feet
And to be baited with the rabble's curse.
Though Birnam Wood be come to Dunsinane,   30
And thou oppos'd, being of no woman born,
Yet I will try the last. Before my body
I throw my warlike shield. Lay on, Macduff,
And damn'd be him that first cries "Hold, enough!"

Exeunt fighting.[†] *Alarms.*

12-13. **I bear…born.** This warning is meant to induce Macduff to cease fighting, for Macbeth does not wish to kill him.—**must not:** according to the decree of fate. 14. **angel:** evil angel, demon.—**still:** always. 15–16. **from…ripp'd:** In Shakespeare's time, a cesarean birth would only have been attempted on a dead or dying woman. Macduff is thus immune from the prophecy either because he was not "born" but "ripp'd" from the womb, because he was born not to a woman, but to a corpse, or both. [A.C.] 18. **my better part of man:** my courage, which is a man's better part; the quality which, more than anything else, makes me a man. Cf. 1.7.46–51; 3.4.58–60, 73, 99, 108. 20. **palter:** deal deceitfully, play fast and loose, equivocate. 21-22. **keep…hope!** fulfill their promise in words but not in the sense we expect. 24. **gaze:** sight, spectacle, show.—**time:** the times, age. 25. **monsters.** The Elizabethans were particularly fond of what we call "side shows." 26. **Painted upon a pole:** i.e., your picture painted on canvas and set up on a pole in front of a showman's booth. 29. **baited:** assailed on all sides, beset—an echo of the bear-baiting figure which Macbeth used in 5.7.1–2. To *bait* is the causative of *bite.* 32-33. **the last:** i.e., strength and valor, which may yet prove stronger than fate. Cf. 3.1.71–72.—**Lay on:** strike hard.

---

†   Shakespeare had Macbeth die offstage, but most film directors are not so restrained. Polanski stages an exhausted and unheroic duel in which Macbeth dies almost by accident. Morrissette has Mac shot as he climbs the roof of his restaurant. And in a famous scene, Washizu is killed not by a Macduff character, but by his own men, who shoot him full of hundreds of arrows. [A.C.]

Retreat and flourish. Enter, with Drum and Colors,
Malcolm, Siward, Ross, Thanes, *and* Soldiers.

MAL.   I would the friends we miss were safe arriv'd.   35

SIW.   Some must go off; and yet, by these I see,
So great a day as this is cheaply bought.

MAL.   Macduff is missing, and your noble son.

ROSS.   Your son, my lord, has paid a soldier's debt.
He only liv'd but till he was a man,   40
The which no sooner had his prowess confirm'd
In the unshrinking station where he fought
But like a man he died.

SIW.   Then he is dead?

ROSS.   Ay, and brought off the field. Your cause of sorrow
Must not be measur'd by his worth, for then   45
It hath no end.

SIW.   Had he his hurts before?

ROSS.   Ay, on the front.

SIW.   Why then, God's soldier be he!
Had I as many sons as I have hairs,
I would not wish them to a fairer death.
And so his knell is knoll'd.

MAL.   He's worth more sorrow,   50
And that I'll spend for him.

SIW.   He's worth no more.
They say he parted well and paid his score,
And so, God be with him. Here comes newer comfort.

Enter Macduff, *with* Macbeth's *head.*

MACD.   Hail, King! for so thou art. Behold where stands
Th' usurper's cursed head. The time is free.   55

---

35. Here a new scene might well be marked. *Retreat* in the stage direction calls for a trumpet signal indicating the defeat of the enemy and checking further pursuit. 36. **go off:** be lost, die.—**by:** to judge by. 39. **paid a soldier's debt:** since every soldier pledges his life to the cause for which he fights. 41. **The which:** i.e., the fact that he had become a man.—**confirm'd:** proved. 42. **the unshrinking station.** The adjective belongs logically to *man*, not to *station*; but such "transference of epithet" is common in the poetry of all periods. 47. **God's solider be he!** God has taken him in the performance of his duty, and so I leave him in God's hands. 50. **knoll'd:** knelled, tolled. 52. **parted well:** departed well, made a good end. The figure is of one who leaves an inn with his bill honestly paid.—**score:** account as scored up. 53. **God be with him!** Good-bye to him! See note on 3.1.44.—**newer comfort:** later news, and good news. 55. **The time:** the world; the people of our time, now delivered from Macbeth's tyranny. Cf.1.5.64–65.

I see thee compass'd with thy kingdom's pearl,
That speak my salutation in their minds;
Whose voices I desire aloud with mine—
Hail, King of Scotland!

ALL.   Hail, King of Scotland!   *Flourish.*

MAL.   We shall not spend a large expense of time   60
Before we reckon with your several loves
And make us even with you. My Thanes and kinsmen,
Henceforth be Earls, the first that ever Scotland
In such an honor nam'd. What's more to do
Which would be planted newly with the time—   65
As calling home our exil'd friends abroad
That fled the snares of watchful tyranny,
Producing forth the cruel ministers
Of this dead butcher and his fiendlike queen,
Who (as 'tis thought) by self and violent hands   70
Took off her life—this, and what needful else
That calls upon us, by the grace of Grace
We will perform in measure, time, and place.
So thanks to all at once and to each one,
Whom we invite to see us crown'd at Scone.†   75

Flourish. Exeunt all.

56. **compass'd:** surrounded.—**pearl:** pearls—a common plural. 60-75. The method of Elizabethan tragedy required that the closing speech should be uttered by the person of highest rank who survived, and this was seldom one of the characters in whom we have taken most interest. Such speeches, therefore, are always rather formal and serve as a kind of epilogue. The lack of a large curtain made the modern fashion of closing a play with a tableau impossible, for the stage had to be cleared. 61. **reckon...loves:** reward the devotion that each of you has shown in my cause.—**loves.** For the plural cf. 3.1.121. 63. **Earls.** Holinshed records that soon after Malcolm's coronation in 1057 "manie of them that before were thanes, were made earles....These were the first earles that haue beene heard of amongst the Scotishmen." 64. **What's more to do:** whatever else remains to be done. 65. **Which would...time:** which the better times that have begun require to be established anew. In plain prose, "any other improvements or reforms that the new order of things requires." For the figure cf. 1.4.28. 66. **our exil'd friends abroad:** our friends who are in exile abroad (like Donalbain in Ireland). 68. **Producing forth:** bringing to light, dragging out of concealment.—**ministers:** agents, instruments. 69. **Butcher** and **fiendlike** are crude terms to apply to Macbeth and his wife, but they correctly express Malcolm's sentiments. Of course he has not the same sympathetic interest in these characters that we have come to feel. 70. **self and violent:** her own violent. Thus we learn that the Doctor's fear that Lady Macbeth would commit suicide was well-founded (5.1.59–61). 71. **Took off.** Cf. 1.7.20.—**what needful else:** whatever else that is necessary. 72. **calls upon us:** demands my attention as King.—**of Grace:** of gracious God. 73. **in measure:** with propriety and decorum, as opposed to the frantic rule of Macbeth.

† Most directors reject Malcolm's claim that good has decisively triumphed over evil. Welles concludes with the Weird Sisters in voice-over, triumphantly cackling "Peace, the charm's wound up," suggesting that even Macbeth's fall was part of their plan. Polanski shows Donalbain (who has earlier looked on jealously at Duncan's favoritism towards Malcolm) sneaking off towards the witches' lair. Kurosawa does not suggest anyone replaces Washizu–the Castle of the Spider's Web is shown deserted and decaying, as voices chant regretfully about human greed. [A.C.]

How to Read *Macbeth* as Performance

Shakespeare's plays are wonderful pieces of literature, full of beautiful images and powerful language. And most often, they are taught as literature, read silently at home, or discussed piece by piece in the classroom. But what a reader needs to know about Shakespeare, and about plays in general, is that plays are not like other types of writing. Plays offer only part of the final product—the dialogue and a few stage directions. Because of this, the best way to fully experience a play is through a performance, live or on film. However, many times seeing a play is not possible, and even when it is, reading is still a valuable experience. It is not always easy to see performances. Some plays aren't staged very often, and when they are they can be expensive. Furthermore, when you see a play, you are seeing the director's version. When you read a play, you can be your own director and imagine the characters and set however you wish. But there are certain techniques all readers must use to get full enjoyment out of reading a Shakespearean play.

Something people often rush past is the list of characters, which is printed at the beginning of the play. It is worth looking at this list to get an idea of the characters. The list for *Macbeth* tells us that Duncan is the King of Scotland, yet the play is not named for him. With many of Shakespeare's plays, the king is the central figure, but here you know that is not true. *Macbeth* is one of Shakespeare's great tragedies and is well known, so even before you start to read, you may be familiar with the story. The play is based on real historical events, which took place around 1040, but Shakespeare was not interested in historical accuracy; instead the play reflects Shakespeare's world.

Despite Shakespeare's indifference to details, costume was very important to his conception of the play. From Act 1, where Banquo says of Macbeth "New honors come upon him/Like our strange garments, cleave not to their mould" (1.3.144–145), to the very end of the play, where Macduff presents Malcolm with the crown of Scotland, clothing and costume is a regular theme. If clothing was important as a theme, how the actual actors dress must also be important. Take a moment and imagine you are the director. How would you like the characters dressed? Would you have them wear early medieval clothing, the elaborate clothing from Shakespeare's time, or something else entirely? In Act 1, most of the men are in armor, since there is a war going on; what does that armor look like? Should the clothing Macbeth wears change as his status and mental state changes?

When you have read the introduction and character list, you have a good basic idea of what the play is about. But all this information will only help you understand it, not make it come alive. In order for that to happen, you need to actively imagine what is happening. You have to create a "theater of the mind." As you read, imagine what the characters look like, how they are dressed and what their surroundings are like. Take the time at the beginning of each scene to imagine what the setting is like. Cast the characters, maybe using your favorite movie stars. Try important speeches in a variety of ways to see which one you like best, and if the different ways can help you uncover different meanings in the scene.

One thing that sets *Macbeth* apart is the supernatural. While many of Shakespeare's plays have some supernatural element, no other tragedy relies so heavily on the supernatural, and only *A Midsummer Night's Dream* places the supernatural front and center. *Macbeth* features, among other things, three witches, a hallucinated dagger and a blood-drenched ghost. Look for a moment at the stage directions in Act 4, scene 1. How would you effectively portray, for example, a bloody child rising out of a cauldron, or a line of ghostly kings? What do the witches look like? How real is the Ghost of Banquo? Reading *Macbeth* requires a very active imagination. Shakespeare meant the play to be visually overwhelming and engaging. When you read the play, try to imagine the scenes in your head, and find the perfect setting to enhance the words.

After you have created the scene in your mind, be alert to what are called *implicit stage directions*. While Shakespeare did not leave many notes about what the actors should do, there are many places where the dialogue refers to actions. These can help guide you in imagining the action. The second scene of *Macbeth* begins with the words, "What bloody man is that?" (1.2.1). Clearly therefore, the man who enters must have some obvious wounds or blood that the audience can see, although exactly how much is up to you. Near the end of the scene, the bloody sergeant says, "I am faint; my gashes cry for help" (1.2.43) and Duncan then orders him helped off stage. This order is further evidence that the sergeant is badly hurt; perhaps he even collapses here.

Sometimes directions can be quite ambiguous, and can alter the audience's perception of the characters. An example of this ambiguity in *Macbeth* comes soon after the murder of Duncan is discovered. As Macbeth is trying to explain his supposedly impassioned murder of the guards (he actually kills them to protect himself), Lady Macbeth says "Help me hence, ho" (2.3.116) and faints. Is she truly fainting here, overcome with the realization of what she and her husband have done, or pretending to faint, to distract the men from Macbeth's implausible explanation? Either way, the characters on stage will react the same, but the audience will have a different view of Lady Macbeth, depending on the actor's choice.

There are other places in *Macbeth* where being an active participant in creating a mental production of the play will help you understand it. There are several scenes where taking the time to read closely and imagine the scene in detail will reveal layers of meaning that just understanding the words will not. These are not, by any means, the only important scenes, but here are some suggestions of places to look closely and imagine yourself as the director.

Macbeth first meets the witches in the third scene, and they promise him he will become king. Does anything in the dialogue suggest that Macbeth has had thoughts about the throne before this, or do the witches create the desire in him? If the latter, in this case is Macbeth merely their puppet? What about Banquo, who is also offered a great future (although a much less clear one)? How does his reaction differ from Macbeth's and what might that difference tell you about each one's character?

In Act 3, scene 4, the Ghost of the murdered Banquo appears at the dinner party, but only Macbeth can see him. Since there are entrances and exits listed for the Ghost, Shakespeare clearly intended an actor to appear onstage as the Ghost. However, since the Ghost has no lines, he could be a figment of Macbeth's guilty imagination (the version starring Ian McKellen indicates that, and films, of course, have the option of leaving the Ghost's reality uncertain). Think about how different choices alter the way the audience understands Macbeth at this, the midpoint of the play.

Right after the murder, at the beginning of Act 2, scene 3, there is a comic scene involving a drunken Porter. Practically, the scene allows the actors playing Macbeth and Lady Macbeth to wash the blood off their hands and change clothes (at the end of 2.2, Lady Macbeth says they must change into their nightgowns, otherwise people will know they have been up and about). Some critics have felt that the scene is a mistake, because it breaks the tension between the murder and discovery scenes. Many others, however, see this scene as special evidence of Shakespeare's genius—taking a necessary pause and creating a piece of black comedy that echoes all the themes and issues in another key. What do you think? The scene is full of comic references contemporary to Shakespeare's time—does any of the humor remain? How would you fill out the verbal humor with physical comedy?

It is in answering questions like those above that understanding how to read a play begins to shade into understanding how to interpret a play. When you play out scenes in your head, and take the time to decide how you think characters should look and dress and act, you begin to see connections that simply aren't apparent from only reading the words on the page. If you take the time to read in this way, not only will you have more fun and understand the play better, you will develop your own interpretation. In fact, you will make the play your own.

TIMELINE

c. 1005: Historical Macbeth (Mac Bethad mac Findláich) born

1040: Historical Macbeth becomes King of Scotland after killing the ruling king, Duncan I, in battle. His marriage to Kenneth III's granddaughter Gruoch strengthens his claim to the throne. By all accounts, his reign is peaceful, equitable, and Christian.

1057: Historical Macbeth killed in battle by Siward.

April 25th, Malcolm III crowned at Scone

1527: Publication of *History of Scotland* by Hector Boece, primary source for Holinshed and a secondary source for Shakespeare

1564: William Shakespeare born in Stratford-upon-Avon to John and Mary Shakespeare

1566: Birth of James Stuart, later James VI of Scotland and I of England

1567: The opening of the Red Lion Playhouse, the first public playhouse in England

1576: James Burbage and friends build The Theater, long thought to be the first public playhouse

1577: Raphael Holinshed first publishes *Chronicles of England, Scotland and Ireland*, Shakespeare's primary source for *Macbeth*

1582: William Shakespeare marries Anne Hathaway.

1583: Birth of Shakespeare's daughter Susanna.

1585: Birth of Shakespeare's twins, son Hamnet and daughter Judith

1592-94: Plague years. Theaters closed. Shakespeare wrote his poems and many of his sonnets during this period.

1594: William Shakespeare and Richard Burbage become sharers in the Lord Chamberlain's Men, a company of actors, when the theaters reopen after the plague. Shakespeare will later become a major shareholder in the theater, and the profit he makes as a shareholder, rather than publication of his plays, is the source of most of his money.

1596: Burial of Hamnet Shakespeare, August 11th, in Statford. Cause of death unknown.

1597:   Publication of *Daemonologie,* a treatise on the supernatural (including witches and ghosts) by the future James I

1603:   Death of Elizabeth I. James VI of Scotland crowned King James I of England.

The Lord Chamberlain's Men, recognized as the premier acting troupe in London, become the King's Men.

1603-6: Probable date of composition for *Macbeth*

1604:   James I creates harsher laws against witchcraft, making any use of witchcraft punishable, rather than (as with previous laws) only acts from malicious intent.

1605-6: Probable date of *Macbeth*'s first performance

1609-16: Probable dates for composition of Thomas Middleton's *The Witch*, source for the interpolated scenes, 3.5 and parts of 4.1

1610:   April 20th, Simon Forman writes in his diary about seeing a performance of *Macbeth.*

c. 1611: Shakespeare gives up writing plays and retires to Stratford.

1616:   April 23rd, Death of William Shakespeare

1623:   *Macbeth* published as part of the First Folio

Topics for Discussion

Study Questions

1. Do you think Macbeth is responsible for his actions, or is he controlled by the witches and/or Lady Macbeth?
2. What is the effect of delaying Macbeth's entrance until 1.3? How does having both the witches and the nobles speak about him contribute to this effect?
3. The major images used in this play are blood, children, and clothing. How do any or all of these images support the main themes of the play?
4. Is Lady Macbeth an unnatural and controlling fiend, a wife who takes her devotion to her husband too far, or something else?
5. What is the purpose of having the Porter scene (2.3) in between Duncan's murder and its discovery?
6. Does the identity of the Third Murderer (3.3) matter? If so, who do you think it is?
7. What is the purpose of the scene in England (4.3) in general, and of Malcolm's false claims about his own nature specifically?
8. How does nature in this play reflect the problems of the human world?
9. J.R.R. Tolkein felt cheated when the prophecy of "Birnham Wood to Dunsinane" turned out to be just branches held by soldiers, and Macduff's mother died before delivering. How do you feel?
10. The witches promised that Banquo's children would inherit the throne, yet at the end of the play Malcolm is crowned king. What kind of ending does this create?

Performance Questions

1. The historical Macbeth lived in the 11th century, but Shakespeare's characters speak and act like nobles of the 17th century. When would you set *Macbeth* and why?
2. How would you portray the witches? How would they look and dress?
3. How realistic should the Ghost of Banquo be?

111

4. Orson Welles cut the play drastically—he even called his version a "charcoal sketch." If you were a director, which scenes would you cut and why?

5. How do you think Lady Macbeth should be portrayed? What should she look like and how should she act?

6. Most of the murders take place off-stage. Aside from the convenience of not having to drag bodies off stage, what is the effect of this?

7. In Roman Polanski's version, the final battle between Macbeth and Macduff is anticlimactic; Macduff kills Macbeth almost by accident. In *Throne of Blood* the Macbeth character is shot by his own men. How would you stage this fight?

8. In both *Men of Respect* and *Throne of Blood* the Macbeth character is no longer the only corrupt character. Instead, the entire world is corrupted by violence and self-interest. How does the common corruption change both the play and the character of Macbeth?

9. *Throne of Blood* not only sets *Macbeth* in another time, but also rewrites the play in Japanese. Is this still *Macbeth*? Why or why not?

10. Watch several versions of *Macbeth*, in whole or part, and discuss which version you think is most effective.

BIBLIOGRAPHY

Adelman, Janet. "'Born of Woman': Fantasies of Maternal Power in *Macbeth*" in *Cannibals, Witches, and Divorce: Estranging the Renaissance*. Ed. Marjorie Garber. Baltimore: Johns Hopkins University Press, 1987, 90-121.

>A feminist interpretation that focuses on Macbeth's question "What's he/That was not born of woman?" and argues that *Macbeth* represents the male desire to escape maternal power and the impossibility of such an escape.

Bradley, A.C. *Shakespearean Tragedy: Lectures on Hamlet, Othello, King Lear, Macbeth*. [1904]. London: St. Martin's Press, 1985.

>Bradley was one of the greatest Shakespearean critics of the early 20th century. He finds *Macbeth* simpler than the other great tragedies, and focuses mainly on the psychology of both Macbeth and Lady Macbeth.

Brooks, Cleanth. "The Naked Babe and the Cloak of Manliness" in *The Well Wrought Urn*. New York: Harcourt, 1947.

>Brooks was one of the creators of New Criticism, a school of literary scholarship that read the texts with great detail and sought to demonstrate how all elements of a work weave together to form a unified whole. Brooks' reading of *Macbeth* shows how two major motifs—children and clothing—support the overall theme.

Brown, John Russell, ed. *Focus on Macbeth*. London: Routledge, 1982.

>A collection of excellent and thoughtful essays from a variety of angles. This collection, although a bit dated, is a wonderful place to begin looking into various approaches to *Macbeth*.

Calderwood, James L. *If It Were Done: Macbeth and Tragic Action*. Amherst: University of Massachusetts Press, 1986.

>Calderwood's study looks at the play as an Aristotelian tragedy, political and social commentary and a response to *Hamlet*. The interweaving of these three themes makes for a rich and valuable reading.

Mullaney, Steven. "Lying Like Truth: Riddle, Representation, and Treason" in *The Place of the Stage: License, Play, and Power in Renaissance England*. Chicago: University of Chicago Press, 1988, 116-34.

> Mullaney weaves the themes of treason, language and spectacle together in viewing *Macbeth* as a case study of the dangers of equivocation and language as theater.

Norbrook, David. "*Macbeth* and the Politics of Historiography" in *Politics of Discourse: The Literature and History of Seventeenth-Century England*. Eds. Kevin Sharpe and Steven Zwicker. Berkeley: University of California Press, 1987, 78-116.

> Norbrook looks at *Macbeth* from a specifically historical perspective, arguing that Shakespeare revised the Scottish histories to make Macbeth more ambiguous than he had previously been presented, and regicide a more complex act.

Sinfield, Alan. "*Macbeth*: History, Ideology and Intellectuals." *Critical Quarterly* 28 (1986): 63-77.

> Sinfield presents a political reading of the violence in the play, suggesting that traditional readings dwell on Macbeth's murders as horrible, but ignore the state-sanctioned violence throughout. Sinfield argues that the play mirrors the way in which citizens are trained to disregard or justify violence perpetrated by the state.

Performances

Anderegg, Michael. *Orson Welles: Shakespeare and Popular Culture*. New York: Columbia University Press, 1999.

> In a larger work about Welles and his versions of Shakespeare, Anderegg provides detailed historical detail about the creation and reception of Welles' *Macbeth* and argues that Welles was making an experimental B movie, which failed with the critics because it could not easily be defined.

Donaldson, Peter S. "Surface and Depth: *Throne of Blood* as Cinematic Allegory" in *Shakespearean Films/Shakespearean Directors*. Boston: Unwin Hyman, 1990.

> Donaldson performs a detailed close reading of the forms used in *Throne of Blood*, especially the spatial elements that Kurosawa controls so tightly.

Jorgens, Jack J. *Shakespeare on Film*. Bloomington: Indiana University Press, 1977.

> Jorgens has three chapters devoted to films of *Macbeth*, versions by Polanski, Welles and others. Although dated in some respects, this seminal work is excellent both for discussing the films as works of art and for providing coherent readings of the films as interpretations of the play itself.

Kliman, Bernice. *Macbeth* (*Shakespeare in Performance*). 2nd edition. Manchester: Manchester University Press, 2004.

    Kliman provides wonderful detailed studies of a variety of performances, including several not mentioned in the introduction. The book covers stage, screen, and television perofrmances and features discussion of international as well as American and British productions.

Naremore, James. "The Walking Shadow: Welles' Expressionist *Macbeth*" in *Literature/Film Quarterly* 1 (1973).

    A detailed study of the way in which Welles reworks *Macbeth* through the visual medium of film, replacing words with images.

FILMOGRAPHY

Note: There are over fifty films and adaptations of *Macbeth*. This bibliography lists the major and most readily available ones. [A.C.]

Macbeth (1948). Dir. Orson Welles. With Orson Welles, Jeanette Nolan, Roddy McDowall. 107 min.

Welles called his film version "a violent charcoal sketch" of the play, because of his drastic cutting and rewriting. The focus is on the conflict between pagan evil and Christian good and, despite the poor Scottish accents Welles insisted everyone adopt, presents a stunning visual representation of Macbeth's decline.

Macbeth (aka *The Tragedy of Macbeth*) (1971). Dir. Roman Polanski. With Jon Finch, Francesca Annis, Martin Shaw. 140 minutes.

Polanski emphasized the corruption of the entire society, beginning with the battle Shakespeare only describes and ending with a shot of Donalbain seeking out the witches. Annis is an unusual Lady Macbeth; she wins Macbeth over with her fragility and youth rather than with an overbearing nature.

Macbeth (1977) Dir. Philip Casson. With Ian McKellen, Judi Dench, John Brown. 146 minutes. DVD release 2004.

DVD extras: Introduction to *Macbeth*; An explanation of the Scottish play (both with McKellen), a timeline of Shakespeare's life and plays.

A stripped down version conceived by Trevor Nunn, this production features two of England's great actors in their prime. Casson's production is especially interesting as all the apparitions take place in Macbeth's mind, and the witches are portrayed as stick figures, directorial choices which leave the focus squarely on Macbeth's decline into madness.

Macbeth (1983). Dir. Jack Gold. With Nicol Williamson, Jane Lapotaire, Ian Hogg. 148 min.

> Part of the BBC Complete Dramatic Works of William Shakespeare, this version offers the fullest text, but suffers from a limited budget and overacting.

Macbeth (1997). Dir. Jeremy Freeston. With Jason Connery, Helen Baxendale, Graham McTavish. 129 minutes

> A low budget but well acted version. Cuts to the secondary characters, however, remove much of their distinctiveness and motivation.

Men of Respect (1991) Dr. William Reilly. With John Turturro, Katherine Borowitz, Dennis Farina. 113 min. DVD release 2003.

> An interesting if uneven Mafia *Macbeth*. Reilly sticks very close to the original plot, a choice which occasionally hampers his actors and the flow of the story. The main change, as with *Throne of Blood*, is that Macbeth is no longer the lone focus of evil, but one corrupted man among many.

Scotland, PA (2001). Dir. Billy Morrissette. With James LeGros, Maura Tierney, Christopher Walken. 104 min. DVD release 2005.

> DVD extras: Director interview and commentary, Insider's Guide to *Scotland, PA*.

> Morrissette relocates the play to a fast food restaurant in the 1970s and half the pleasure of the film is catching all the in-jokes (Duncan Donuts). The other half is realizing how dramatically our own reactions change when the crimes are committed by pathetic fast food employees rather than kings and nobles.

Star Trek: Conscience of the King (1966) Episode #1.13. Dir. Gerd Oswald. With William Shatner, Leonard Nimoy, Arnold Moss.

> Although this episode has more connections to *Hamlet* than *Macbeth*, the central theme of the guilty conscience is similar and the episode features a partial performance, the "Arcturian Macbeth," in which the audience actually sees Macbeth murder the sleeping Duncan.

Throne of Blood aka *The Castle of the Spider's Web* (Japanese title *Kumonosu jô*) (1957). Dir. Akira Kurosawa. With Toshirô Mifune, Isuzu Yamada, Takashi Shimura. 105 min. DVD release 2003

> DVD extras: Audio Commentary by Japanese-film expert Michael Jeck, two alternative subtitle translations.

> Kurosawa's brilliant rendition of *Macbeth* uses elements of Noh traditional theater and portrays Macbeth's conflict as well as any English version, and better than most, although, as with *Men of Respect*, the Macbeth character is only one corrupt man in a society built on violence and personal greed.